Northamptonshire

A Portrait in Pen & Ink

The Village Centre, Hannington.

1. HANNINGTON

Hannington is a quiet, tiny place, more a hamlet than a village, for there is no pub, shop or Post Office. In days gone by it consisted of a number of farm buildings, farmhouses and labourers' cottages. Today there are still some farmhouses and a few of the cottages, the Old Bakehouse, the Old Forge and the former rectory still exist as modernised houses. More than half the village dwellings are of more recent construction.

About midway between Northampton and Kettering and a mile to the west of the A43, Hannington has two vague connections in history, both connected with the Church of St Peter and St Paul. It is thought that the church was founded by a cell of the Gilbertine monks of Sempringham in Lincolnshire; they were the only English order of monks and included both male and female members. The unusual division of the nave in the church by an arcade of thirteenth-century round columns was designed to separate the men from the women. It is felt that this almost unique feature, which makes the church so interesting, is connected with St Gilbert of Sempringham.

The other connection is with Great Doddington, as rumour has it that Thomas a Becket took refuge at Hardwater Mill, beside the River Nene, following his escape from Northampton Castle. He is also supposed to have spent the night at the church in Hannington. Presumably this was also on his escape route.

Finally, I suspect that it is little-known that Bishop Francis Godwin is said to have been born in Hannington. Elizabeth I made him Bishop of Llandaff, then Bishop of Hereford. He is credited with writing the story 'The Man in the Moon', and he became something of a Jules Verne of his time. He was a man who saw a time in the future when man would fly, survey the heavens and have access to instantaneous communication. Francis Godwin is buried at Whitbourne in Herefordshire.

Northamptonshire

A PORTRAIT IN PEN & INK

CLIVE HOLMES

The
History
Press

For Kathleen, Deborah and Malcolm.

The preparation for this book has been a lengthy but interesting process.
At all stages I have enjoyed the company of my wife and thank her for being my navigator, advisor, critic and editor.

First published 2010

The History Press
The Mill, Brimscombe Port
Stroud, Gloucestershire, GL5 2QG
www.thehistorypress.co.uk

© Clive Holmes, 2010

British Library Cataloguing in Publication Data.
A catalogue record for this book is available from the British Library.

ISBN 978 0 7524 5351 4

Typesetting and origination by The History Press
Printed in India by Nutech Print Services

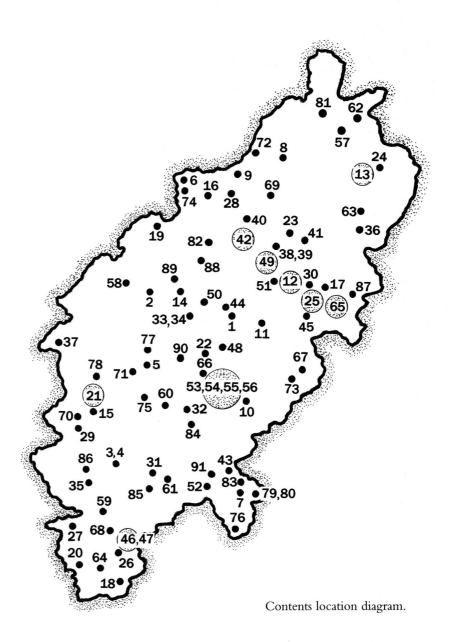

Contents location diagram.

Contents

Cottages at the entrance to Cottesbrooke Hall.

2. COTTESBROOKE

At Cottesbrooke, these cottages, one slate-roofed and one thatched, stand surrounded by beautiful trees at the entrance to the well-known Cottesbrooke Hall. Just beyond the gateway, the visitor enters the magnificent gardens which surround this fine eighteenth-century building. The hall is situated about ten miles north of Northampton and was, during the nineteenth century, home to the Empress of Austria.

The village itself retains much 'old world' charm and contains numerous dwellings, large and small, similar in appearance to those in this illustration.

About 1150, an order of monks was founded at Laon in France. The same order flourished during medieval times, not too far from today's village of Cottesbrooke, and the 'White Canons', as they were known, were dissolved by Henry VIII during the Dissolution of the Monasteries. Locally there is a field in which there is a spring, which has in the past been referred to as 'Monks Well' or 'St Norbert's Field', for it was St Norbert who founded the original order.

The Church of All Saints dates mainly from 1220, but like many village churches, it has been developed during later years. Inside it has a three-tier pulpit, certainly quite unique, and a pew for the squire is in the organ loft of all places, and is complete with its own fire grate.

6

Introduction & Bibliography

Alittle less than 1,000 sq. miles of Middle England is covered by the small and little-known county of Northamptonshire. A county of spires, squires and forests is how it has frequently been referred to, and yet it is to a great extent England in a nutshell.

Within the county is architecture to please the eye. Cottages, houses, fine churches and numerous great mansions are constructed from a wide variety of local building materials. Here is history spanning the time from the Iron Age through Roman, Saxon, Norman and Elizabethan periods to the English Civil War. Famous events and battles have taken place here and kings, lords and earls have left their mark upon the county. Here too the people had to earn a living from agriculture, sheep farming, quarrying, leatherwork and iron and steel production.

With this background as my inspiration, I was commissioned in 2004 by the *Northamptonshire Chronicle & Echo* to produce a series of pen and ink illustrations, together with a complimentary text. The series was entitled 'Around the County'.

This book, my second on Northamptonshire, is a selection taken from that series. It ran for four years, during which time I travelled extensively, sketching, photographing and studying the history of the county. It does not pretend to be an authoritative work on Northamptonshire, but simply a portrait in pen and ink of this part of Middle England.

Billing, C., *Northamptonshire Curiosities.* (Dovecote Press, 1993)

Gould, Jack, *Northamptonshire: Shire County Guide.* (Shire Publications, 1988)

Jeremiah, Josephine, *The River Nene: A Pictorial History.* (Phillimore & Co. Ltd, 2003)

Mee, Arthur, *The Kings England: Northamptonshire.* (Hodder & Stoughton, 1975)

Noble, T., *Exploring Northamptonshire.* (Meridan Books, 1987)

Noble, T., *Exploring Parish Churches in Northamptonshire.* (Jema Publications, 1999)

Noble, T., *Northamptonshire: A Portrait in Colour.* (Dovecote Press, 1995)

Northamptonshire Village Book. (WI & Countryside Books, 1989)

Royal Northamptonshire. (Northamptonshire Leisure & Libraries, 1989)

Stigner, J., *Photographers' Britain.* (Alan Sutton, 1992)

3. CANONS ASHBY

Situated close to a bend on the B4525 road and about ten miles from Banbury is the lovely Canons Ashby House and the Church of St Mary. Both buildings have been in the care of the National Trust since 1980 and have required substantial amounts of money to save them from ruin.

The house, connected to the church by way of a footpath, was acquired, together with the estate and the priory, in 1538 by Sir John Cope. About thirteen years later, his daughter Elizabeth married John Dryden and from that time until the late 1700s, the house was extended a little at a time. Since then, little has changed; thus today's house is virtually the same as it was 250 years ago.

It is not a huge house, but one that the visitor can enjoy and have the feeling that it was a family home. There are the usual paintings of family members and assorted heirlooms, but nothing too ostentatious. The entrance to the house is by the imposing great hall and the other rooms contain examples of Jacobean plasterwork and wall paintings. For me, however, the kitchen is one of the most interesting of many great houses.

Canons Ashby House.

The west front, The Augustinian Priory, Canons Ashby.

4. ST MARY'S CHURCH, CANONS ASHBY

This magnificent west end of the former Augustinian priory dominates the narrow road at Canons Ashby. Close by stand just a few cottages and the odd farm, together with Canons Ashby House.

The church was originally part of a priory founded in 1150 by canons of the Augustine Order and the remains of this once huge building, dedicated to St Mary, date from the thirteenth and fourteenth centuries. During the English Civil War, the Parliamentarian forces took refuge in the tower and only escaped being forced out by the Royalists when reinforcements from Northampton drove off the King's men. The tower still bears shot marks from this encounter.

Some have likened this view to Lincoln Cathedral, for the great doorway has eight columns with ornamental capitals, above which is the huge 400-year-old window, and there are no less than eleven arches along the front of the building.

Once inside, it becomes apparent that there is little left today of what must have been a glorious place before the Dissolution of the Monasteries. A doorway leads from the north aisle into the tower and two high arches separate the nave from the aisle. The unusual font dates from the fourteenth century and understandably there are a number of monuments to the Dryden family, who resided at Canons Ashby House.

5. GREAT BRINGTON

Here, from the left, is the Althorpe Coaching Inn, the Post Office and cottages in a most attractive stone terrace beneath an almost completely thatched roof. Understandably, this row of buildings forms the hub of this small village, while across the road from the inn are a few modern houses.

Since the death of Diana, Princess of Wales, Great Brington has become a popular tourist attraction with its close proximity to Althorpe. The inn has, I suspect, been little changed for generations and the Post Office is tiny and quaint.

The church stands on an outcrop of land at the edge of the village and commands beautiful countryside views to the north. It was built about 1200 with many additions being made during the fourteenth and fifteenth centuries, but the main interest in the church are the monuments to the Spencer family in the chapel of that name. The ostentatious, full length effigies of family members are said to be among the finest in this part of England.

The brothers Lawrence and Robert Washington, sons of Lawrence, the builder of Sulgrave Manor and forefather of George Washington, first President of the United States of America, both have tombs here. It is also said that whilst a prisoner at Holdenbury House, Charles I took communion here in 1647.

The Althorpe Coaching Inn left, Post Office centre and cottages, Great Brington.

6. WESTON BY WELLAND

Almost at the border with Leicestershire, Weston by Welland is just to the north-east of Market Harborough, jutting out into the Welland Valley. From just behind the village, fine views can be had of Northamptonshire, Leicestershire and Rutland.

The village straddles the B664 road between Sutton Bassett and Medbourne, across the border in Leicestershire, and consists of a pleasant mixture of buildings of varying ages. The village first had a church dedicated to St Mary during the thirteenth century, but it was largely rebuilt as recently as 1866 and followed the original plan. The Revd Samuel Danby, together with some of the local landowners, funded the structure themselves and they made a very worthwhile job of it. High up on the battlemented tower are a series of carved heads, but good eyesight or a pair of binoculars are necessary to pick out the detail.

For generations, the sons of the Danby family, who resided in the large house opposite the church, became the village vicars right up to the twentieth century. Today the house is a private dwelling. The old village school, built during the late 1800s, is also a private house and the public house, formerly known as the Carpenters Arms, was a two-storey building, having a third storey added in order to accommodate the Irish labourers who laid the nearby railway line. Weston's village station was about a mile from the village and the remains of the former rail route, which ran toward Oadby in Leicestershire, can still be seen today.

Weston by Welland

The Old Mill, Potterspury.

7. POTTERSPURY

Prior to the twelfth century, it would seem that the areas surrounding the village were referred to as 'places where pears are grown' and consequently became known as 'pyrige'. During the twelfth century, potteries were developed here and a number of sites uncovered during more recent times have led to the belief that the names 'potter' and 'pears' were joined, hence the present village is known as Potterspury. However, a settlement of some kind must have existed here hundreds of years earlier, for it is known that a church was built here about twenty years after the Battle of Hastings. Today's church is dedicated to St Nicholas and in the main was constructed during the thirteenth and fourteenth centuries, but it still has Norman carvings on the capitals of the pillars in the north arcade.

Lying only a short distance from Stony Stratford and on the old Roman road, Watling Street, in days gone by the village would have been surrounded by the great forest of Wittlebury. It was within this vicinity that Michael Harrison established the foundations of his Independent Church in 1690. The church was further developed during the 1700s by John Heywood, who formed an unlikely friendship with the Duke of Grafton, who resided at Wakefield Lodge.

The 2nd Duke of Grafton had acquired a hunting lodge a mile or so to the south of Potterspury as early as 1748 and it was he who employed William Kent to build his house for him. Capability Brown was brought in to design the gardens and create its superb water gardens. As recently as 1918, this fine estate was divided up and sold off. As for the people of the village, they had for generations been employed on the land and as little as 150 years ago, it was known that female workers as young as five years of age were employed as lacemakers. Schools, however, were established in the second half of the 1800s for the youngsters of Potterspury.

Finally, it is interesting to note that during the Second World War, a mill which had functioned locally for generations was eventually closed down and forty years later the buildings were developed as private dwellings.

Deene Park.

8. DEENE PARK

This is indeed a fine house; not the largest and certainly not the most flamboyant, but one of the most interesting in the county. As a schoolboy, I well remember those tragic and noble words of the famous poem 'The Charge of the Light Brigade'. It is only when I retired to Northamptonshire that I learned that Deene Park was the home of the 7th Earl of Cardigan, who led the charge. He was the victim of a terrible misunderstanding of orders in the confusion of battle, but it was not his fault. He returned home to find himself a hero of the Crimean War. He later died in a riding accident, when he fell from the same horse that had carried him at Balaklava in 1854.

The house nestles amidst the trees beside the Willow Brook and is situated to the west of the A43 road, just north-west of Corby. Primarily a sixteenth-century house, it incorporates a former manor dating from medieval times and has been the home of the Brudenell family since 1514. Around the time of the Norman Conquest, the Manor of Deene was visited on occasions by the Abbot of Westminster, as it was in the ownership of Westminster Abbey. By 1215 it was let to Sir Ivo de Deene, who provided hospitality once a year for the abbot. The house certainly has a full and interesting history, and contains stained glass from the seventeenth century, family portraits and uniforms and memorabilia of the Crimean War.

9. ROCKINGHAM

'An ideal place from which to subdue my new kingdom,' thought William the Conqueror, so he ordered that a substantial stronghold was to be built at Rockingham. With its far reaching views across the Welland Valley, the castle has stood here ever since and in 1095 it was such an important place that the Great Council of Rockingham was held here.

It was converted into a fine house by Edward Watson, who had obtained a lease of Rockingham from Henry VIII. Later in 1695, Sir Lewis Watson bought the freehold from James I. It remained in Royalist hands until the Civil War when it was taken by Cromwell's troops. During the fighting many of the buildings were damaged and the attractive village that we know today, lying below the castle, dates from the late 1600s. Formerly a market town, the village was greatly updated by the Watson family during the nineteenth century. The old school building, next to the village store, was opened in 1844 and functioned for about 100 years. More recently it was used as the village hall.

Seen here is the view from the bottom of Rockingham's Main Street, close to the border with Leicestershire. On each side of the road are beautiful stone dwellings, a number of which have thatched roofs. The castle can just be seen from this point overlooking the village on the top left.

Main Street, Rockingham.

10. LITTLE HOUGHTON

Just to the east of Northampton is the handsome old village of Little Houghton. Here, dating back to well before the birth of Christ, there was a place to cross the River Nene and by AD 800, a mill was operating close by. During later centuries, the Romans came and, being aware of the strategic importance of the ford, they developed a settlement at Little Houghton. About forty years after the Norman Conquest the Chamberlain to Henry I, William de Houghton, constructed an early form of castle close to the river in order to protect the mill and the ford. It would have been of motte and bailey design, and later the mound became known as Clifford Hill.

Alas, in 1333 almost all the village was wiped out by fire. By comparison, a later fire in 1780 only destroyed a quarter of the properties of Little Houghton. In spite of these setbacks, the village we see today is almost entirely protected by a conservation order. Many of the old stone cottages, houses and farm buildings date from the seventeenth and eighteenth centuries. The credit for the refurbishing and rebuilding of many of the village properties during earlier centuries must surely go to three families who in turn held the lordship of the manor between them since shortly after the coming of the Normans. The Houghtons, the Wards and, finally, the Smyths are in many ways responsible for the way the village looks today.

At the centre of the village, right beside the crossroads, is the Post Office with the old village stocks still standing to the right of it. An inscription tells that these stocks date from 1835, and the last man to be put in an earlier set of stocks was William Burcott, in 1833, for drunken behaviour and for ill treatment of his wife.

The Post Office, Little Houghton.

The old School, Schoolhouse and the church of St Leonard, Hardwick.

11. HARDWICK

The tiny hamlet of Hardwick lies hidden amidst the fields and woodlands of a landscape typical of Northamptonshire's countryside. A short distance to the east of the busy A43 and a few miles from Wellingborough, it is reached by a series of narrow, twisting lanes. Peaceful in its remoteness, it has changed little for generations and has escaped development, probably due to the fact that it has no major road access.

At the time of Domesday, it was the home to twenty-five people; by the nineteenth century the number had increased by five times, but today there are barely a dozen houses here.

The fine manor house is now a farm and a 'pick your own' fruit farm, but in centuries gone by it was the home of the Knights Templar and has bay windows that date from the fourteenth century. During the early seventeenth century, Sir Francis Nicolls resided here. He was the governor of the fort at Tilbury at the time of the Spanish Armada, when Elizabeth I reviewed the troops who had massed there to resist the invasion by the forces of the Duke of Palma. A small wall-monument to Sir Francis, who died in 1621, is in the church and depicts him with his family.

St Leonard's Church, seen on the left of my illustration, was constructed about 1200. The battlemented tower, together with most of the remainder of the church, dates from the thirteenth century, with a clerestory being added a century later. The font, from the same period, is most unusual in design, having the bowl set within six arches, each arch having the appearance of a window. The pulpit is also unusual, being made of Italian marble, and is nineteenth century in origin.

To the right is the former village school and school house. Constructed during the Victorian period, as many village schools were, it has for many years been used as the village hall.

Church Street, Burton Latimer.

12. BURTON LATIMER

In Church Street in Burton Latimer stands this fine, old, limestone building with four stone mullion windows beneath a roof of thatch. Above the front doorway is a stout gable with the inscription: 'THIS HOVSE WAS BVILT 1622 THE FRESCHOOL WAS FOUNDED BY THOMAS BVRBANKE AND MARGARET HIS WIFE 1587'. Until the 1960s the building still housed a school, but since the closure of the school it has become a private residence. Most of the neighbouring stone houses date from the eighteenth century, while a few are considerably older.

Evidence suggests that as early as the Bronze Age a settlement existed close by, and much later a Romano-British settlement was developed to the south-west of present-day Burton Latimer, close to the River Ise.

During Saxon times, the Earl Ralp owned the village of Burtone. The name was derived from the Saxon description of 'burh tun', which meant a fortified farmstead, which is just about what it was at that time. Just a couple of years after the Norman invasion of 1066, this former Saxon manor became the property of the Norman Lord of the Manor, Guy de Reinbuedcurt.

Latimer Hall, on the Kettering Road, was built during the early part of the seventeenth century and is said to stand on the original site of the former manor house. A local legend from the eleventh century tells of the wicked Lord Seagrave abducting the Lady Isabel de Latimer, who was betrothed to Sir Hugh Neville. The gallant Sir Hugh tried to rescue his true love but both he and Isabel were killed. Her ghost is said to haunt the place where she died, the ford at the bottom of Barton Hill.

By 1849, carpet weaving provided employment for many of the townsfolk and by 1857, the coming of the Midland Railway, together with the production of leather goods, meant that the town expanded considerably. The population increased tremendously during this period, which resulted in the development of many streets of red brick houses to accommodate the work force.

Alumasc, a company manufacturing brewery equipment, is one of the present major employers, the other being the producers of the famous breakfast cereal in the yellow packet, Weetabix.

The Market Place, Oundle.

13. OUNDLE

Oundle is one of the most attractive of England's small country towns and is positioned on a wide bend in the River Nene. It is widely known for its public school, which is housed in impressive buildings in different parts of the town, and for its seventeenth- and eighteenth-century stone buildings which are admired by all who visit. It also possesses a number of handsome old inns, private houses, cottage-filled side streets and two fine, old churches, one of medieval origin and the other constructed during the nineteenth century.

The most recent of these churches, the Jesus Church, stands at the junction of the roads from Stoke Doyle and Benefield. Designed by Sir Arthur Blomfield in 1879, this Catholic church is built in a striking Gothic style. St Peter's stands between North Street and New Street on the site of an earlier Saxon church and dominates the skyline with its elegant steeple rising from a sturdy tower which can be seen for many a mile across the water meadows of the surrounding countryside.

Pictured here is the town's marketplace when looking west. To the right is the seventeenth-century Oundle Bookshop, with its charming Georgian shop front behind a handsome Doric colonnade. On the first floor are six windows, with six dormers protruding from the roof. At both ends of the roof are pairs of tall, handsome chimneys. On an island in the middle of the marketplace and on the left in my illustration, stands the former Town Hall, now an estate agents office. It was constructed during the early nineteenth century, having two storeys with stout gables and a charming oriel window on its west end.

IN THINGS TRANSITORY RESTETH

Lamport Hall.

14. LAMPORT

Close to where the main road from Brixworth to Market Harborough is joined by the High Street, Lamport stands on high ground commanding fine views across the surrounding countryside. In the days of coach travel, this was said to be the bleakest point of the whole journey between York and London.

The tiny village of Lamport consists of little more than a couple of large modern houses, a few cottages, a farm, the handsome rectory of 1730, the church, the Swan restaurant and, of course, Lamport Hall. The dignified hall makes a fine subject for pen and ink illustration amidst the bare trees of early spring.

Back in 1560, John Isham bought the manor of Lamport. From 1654 to 1657, the hall was rebuilt for Sir Justinian Isham, who was a Royalist during the English Civil War. John Webb, the son-in-law of Inigo Jones, was the builder. During 1730 and 1740, extensions were added to the north and south sides of the building by Smith's of Warwick.

The house is well-known throughout the county for its fine furniture and collection of paintings, mainly of family members. In the past, this great house also housed one of the finest collections of Elizabethan books in England.

Newnham.

15. Newnham

Newnham stands close to the border with Warwickshire. The village sits at the edge of the Northamptonshire Uplands, with Arbury Hill and the source of the River Nene close by.

The village church, dedicated to St Michael and All Angels, dates from the fifteenth century and, as my illustration shows, it has an open-based tower, which is rare in Northamptonshire. The arches form an open air porch which leads into the church. The ropes for the bells pass through spaces in the roof of the porch and the bells were rung in the open air.

Close to the church, in the house with stone gables, Thomas Randolph was born. He was baptised here in 1605. Residing in the village, he became a poet but was little-known nationally. He died whilst visiting his friend William Stafford at Blatherwycke and is buried there.

Better known hereabouts is the Welshman, Romer Williams, who lived at Newnham Hall during the late 1800s and bought the former village pub, the Bakers Arms, after it had been damaged by fire. He had the building completely refurbished and today the village's only pub, situated beside the village green and now renamed the Romer Arms, still serves refreshments.

The old School and the church of St Botolph, Stoke Albany.   C. Holmes

16. STOKE ALBANY

William de Albini became Lord of the Manor here during the thirteenth century and it is from his name that Albany is derived. He built himself a fine new manor house, and at the same time redesigned the village by giving it four parallel streets. Whilst the manor house, standing in Ashley Road, is without doubt a fine old building, the Old Hall house, parts of which date from the twelfth century, is the oldest of the village's buildings. It stands to the left of the church, just out of view of my illustration.

Shown here is the former school, now the Village Hall, built in 1871 on part of the land that belonged to the Old Hall house. It is typical of many schools built in England during the Victorian period, and it reminds me of the primary school that I attended as a child in the village of Bidston, on the Wirral Peninsula.

The village church, beyond the chestnut trees, can only be seen from this viewpoint during the winter months as the foliage blocks the view at other times of the year. St Botolph was a monk who became the patron saint of travellers, and it is he to whom the church is dedicated. The tower, with its grotesque gargoyles at each corner, was embattled during the fifteenth century. Over the porch is a sundial, above which, on a wooden tablet, a notice requires men entering the church to scrape the mud from their footwear and women to remove their patterns.

In the churchyard is buried Lord Denman, who died in the parish in 1854 after a quite remarkable life. He was born in 1779 to a Nottinghamshire family and educated at the Norfolk school of Mrs Barbauld, later moving to Eton. He became Chief Justice Denman and also Solicitor General. He joined Lord Brougham in defending Queen Caroline and persuaded Parliament to withdraw the divorce bill. In later life, he spoke out for the freedom of slaves.

All Saints church and Ivy Cottage, Great Addington.

17. GREAT ADDINGTON

To the east of Burton Latimer, the village of Great Addington stands along the Irthlingborough to Woodford road. Long before the Romans came here, evidence has proved that earlier settlements existed to the south-east, and an area known today as Shooters Hill is where a number of human skeletons were found in 1847.

As always, the close proximity to the river was essential for survival and transportation, so the stream that flowed into the River Nene was important for the existence of the village. During the fourteenth century, plague and famine sent the population into decline and while a number of local villages became deserted, Great Addington, or 'Addington Magna' as it was previously known, survived.

The de Vere name is synonymous with the diamond industry, and the family have been associated with the village since 1125 when one Audrey de Vere resided at the manor. Over the following generations, the manor and all of its lands passed down to Henry de Vere, who died in 1516. He had survived the War of the Roses, fought at Bosworth Field and is commemorated by an alabaster figure in the church.

Today's manor house, said to be of Jacobean origin, stands across the road from the church, shielded from view by high walls and hedges. Parts of the building date from the seventeenth century, with later extensions being made during Victorian times.

The centre of the village is undoubtedly the Church of All Saints and it makes a great visual impact, with Ivy Cottage to the right. It is thought that a Norman church once stood on the same site, but today only the Norman doorway, with its outer arch of chevrons at the porch entrance, exists from this period. The tower was built in 1350 and inside the nave, great Norman stones support the columns of the arcades, above which the clerestory dates from the fifteenth century. The chancel dates from the thirteenth to the fifteenth centuries, and within the North Chapel is the tomb of Henry de Vere.

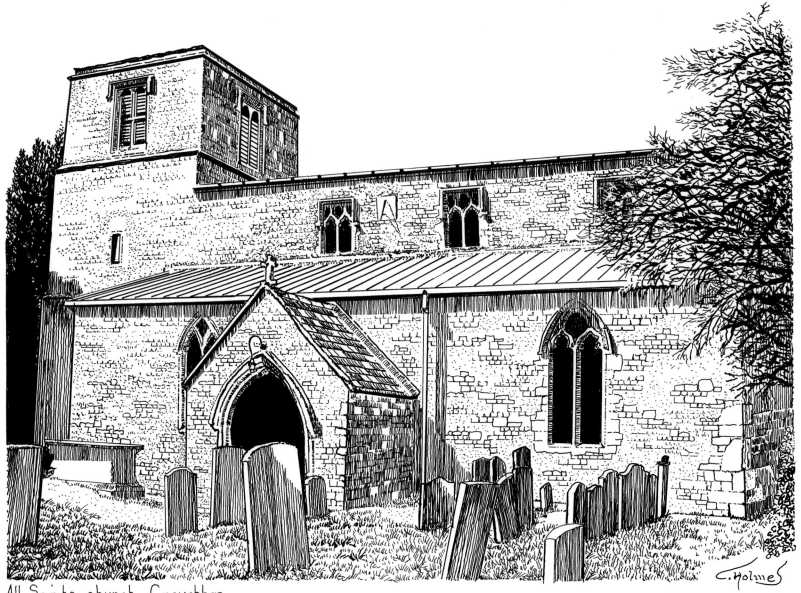

All Saints church, Croughton.

18. CROUGHTON

One of the most southerly villages in the county, Croughton sits close to the borders of Buckinghamshire and Oxfordshire. The village, consisting of a mixture of architectural styles in stone and brick, still has a village store, Post Office, public house and village school serving the local residents.

The old Church of All Saints is situated just to the south of the High Street and is accessed via Church Lane. The building itself is attractive because of its simplicity, but the church became famous when, during restoration work in the last century, an amazing collection of wall paintings were exposed. The Croughton Pictures, as they became known, almost cover the walls of the nave. It is understood that they were painted using egg white and ochre during the early part of the fourteenth century, when they must have been a spectacular sight. No less than thirty-six biblical scenes were uncovered, and it is therefore no wonder that this little church of simple design became as famous as it did all those years ago.

East Farndon Manor.

19. EAST FARNDON

Like many of the old villages of Northamptonshire, East Farndon was recorded at the time of Domesday in 1086. A stone in a nearby field is known locally as the 'Judith Stone', a reminder that at that time local land was owned by Countess Judith of Huntingdon.

More recently, following the Battle of Naseby at the close of the English Civil War, this rather isolated village was chosen as the best place to bring the King's dispatches for safe keeping. I suspect that at that time there was very little here and it was felt that for security reasons it was a good choice.

East Farndon is situated a couple of miles south of Market Harborough and close to the border of Northamptonshire and Leicestershire. It consists of a mixture of old and new houses sprinkled along each side of the main street as it climbs up the long hill. From the top of the hill, close to the church, there are fine views across rolling farmland to Market Harborough in the distance.

The Church of St John the Baptist dates mainly from the fourteenth and fifteenth centuries, and contains an unusual brass; it is a portrait of Daniel Halford, who was a rector during the seventeenth century, together with a laurel wreath, hourglass and skull. A further memorial to another past rector is a window depicting Faith, Hope and Charity. A slab of slate commemorates the Lee family, who resided locally from 1693 until 1804.

For me, however, the most attractive building in the village is in Back Street. It is a small, stone manor house with the date 1664 carved on it, and it still retains its fine stone mullioned bay windows. It is indeed a noble looking dwelling.

Kings Sutton.

20. KINGS SUTTON

Kings Sutton sits in the far south-west of Northamptonshire, right beside the River Cherwell and about as close to Oxfordshire as you can get. During the Dark Ages, our county was part of Mercia and was ruled by Penda, the last of the pagan kings, who, it is believed, had a household here. As the story goes, his grandson, Rumbold, was born of Christian parents and only lived for three days, but was able to preach Christianity. Needless to say, he became Saint Rumbold and hundreds of years later local springs were named after him.

The very heart of this large, attractive, ironstone village is aptly named 'The Square'. The Church of St Peter and St Paul stands on the west side of this grassy centrepiece and close by is the large house known as Lovells, next to which are a couple of pretty thatched cottages. Facing Lovells is the manor house with the nineteenth-century stocks preserved behind an iron fence. Next to the manor is the fine, part timber-framed building shown in my illustration. This was the courthouse during the sixteenth century. To the left and beyond the tree is the village pub, the White Horse.

Within the criss-cross of adjacent narrow streets there is a mixture of architectural styles, with many of the older houses being constructed of locally quarried ironstone. A number of them still display the insurance badges from days gone by.

During the late seventeenth century, natural springs were discovered at Astrop and it became known as St Rumbold's Well. It was claimed that all manner of ailments could be cured by 'taking the waters'. The popularity lasted for about 100 years but as Leamington Spa became fashionable, St Rumbold's decreased in popularity.

21. DAVENTRY

The history of Daventry stretches back to prehistoric times, when one of the largest hill forts in Middle England existed here. At 650ft above sea level, Borough Hill is said to have been the third largest hill fort in the land, for it was two miles around and enclosed about 150 acres.

By about AD 1108, a priory was moved from Preston Capes to a new site at Daventry, and after a difficult period of early development, it had grown in size and stature by the thirteenth century. During this period, the early town had also grown and thrived, mainly through farming.

Much more recently, during the English Civil War, Charles I stayed at the old hostelry known as the Wheatsheaf Inn and his army camped at Borough Hill the night before the Battle of Naseby.

During the days of coach travel, the town was well-positioned as a staging post, being twelve miles to the west of Northampton, twenty miles from Warwick and twenty miles from Coventry. By the late 1700s, mail coaches were clattering their way through Daventry's streets en route to London, Liverpool, Chester and numerous other destinations. About this time, the manufacture of footwear was booming in Daventry and a little later, with the development of the Grand Junction Canal wharves at Long Buckby and Braunston, further opportunities in transportation presented themselves to local manufacturers.

Whilst present-day Daventry has seen much housing and industrial development during the last twenty-five years or so, there is still some evidence of the older properties around the town centre. In the High Street there are still some old ironstone houses and the former Grammar School of 1600 still exists in New Street.

Shown here are two features of Daventry's Market Square. To the right is the fine, eighteenth-century Moot Hall, minus its dome-shaped cupola, which was removed for safety reasons. Grade II listed and now on English Heritage's buildings at risk register, until recent years the Moot Hall housed the town museum and Tourist Information Centre; alas, they are no longer there. To the left is the very elaborate memorial to Edmund Charles Burton, who was a prominent figure in the town's affairs during the late 1800s.

The Burton Memorial and the Moot Hall, Daventry.

Finally, two people who were born in Daventry during the seventeenth century should be mentioned. The first, known simply as John Smith, died at the age of ninety. John Smith became well-known for his engravings of portraits and religious depictions of the period. He is buried at St Peter's in Northampton. The other native of the town was Henry Holland, who wasted his life in a failed attempt to restore in England the authority of the Pope.

22. BOUGHTON

This attractive row of terraced houses in Butchers Lane at Boughton faces the gentle slope of the village's main street.

The present village was developed after the Black Death and consists of a picturesque mixture of cottages, houses, the former rectory and the thatched house of 1574, which was at one time the Lion public house. The Church of St John the Baptist was a chantry chapel during the sixteenth century, being founded around 1545. The centre of the village is now protected by a preservation order.

One of the most important annual horse fairs in this part of England was held in Boughton from 1351 until 1916. It lasted three days and after a church service on the feast day of St John the Baptist, livestock, agricultural goods and property were sold.

Butchers Lane, Boughton.

Boughton House.

23. BOUGHTON HOUSE

The magnificent Boughton House is shown as seen in the distance from the A43 road, just to the south of Geddington. Its origins go back 500 years, but the building we see today was mainly constructed during the seventeenth century.

During the time of Henry VIII, Sir Edward Montagu became the guardian of the young Edward VI. He was well rewarded by the King following the Dissolution of the Monasteries, receiving many properties in Northamptonshire, and it was Sir Edward who founded the house. However, it was not until 1683 that real progress was made by Ralph, the 1st Duke of Montagu. He seems to have made his fortune by marrying rich widows; first the Countess of Northumberland and, following her death, the Duchess of Albemarle. He was at one time the Ambassador to France and was greatly influenced by Versailles. During this time, he collected furniture and other fine things with which to fill his beautiful home. Consequently, the house today contains a heady mixture of furniture, tapestries, paintings, arms, silver, porcelain and needlework too numerous to mention here.

His son was known as 'John the Planter', for he seemed to have a natural ability to create beautiful gardens. Together with his father, he gave the house two large courtyards and diverted streams in order to fill great lakes, cascades and pools. The historic avenues of trees were originally laid out in 1700 by the Dutch gardener Van der Meulen, together with a canalised river and lakes.

Today, Boughton House is the home of the Duke of Buccleuch and Queensbury. Both the house and grounds are Grade II listed and, understandably, the house is considered to be one of the finest in Europe, with the north front giving the impression of being a French chateau. Beyond this front, however, is a very English structure almost like a village of its own. The building has seven courtyards, twelve entrances and fifty-two chimneys, with over an acre of Collyweston slate on its roof.

The Chequered Skipper, Ashton.

24. ASHTON

Ashton lies just across the River Nene to the east of Oundle and is both picturesque and unusual. It was rebuilt as a model village laying beneath thatched roofs in 1900 for Charles, the second son of Lord Rothschild, at a time when there was a great interest in developing houses with up-to-date facilities in close proximity to nature. Developments of note around this period took place at Port Sunlight, the home of Sunlight soap, and at Bournville, famous for Cadbury's chocolate. Here at Ashton, the development was on a much smaller scale, but was nevertheless acclaimed as a big step forward, for while the houses had a certain Tudor appearance, they had modern amenities such as inside bathrooms.

Charles Rothschild became a great expert on fleas and was acknowledged as one of the foremost entomologists of his day. He founded the Society for the Promotion of Nature Reserves, which later became known as the Royal Society for Nature Conservation.

The Chequered Skipper is a most unusual name for a public house, but here in Ashton I have no doubt that its title has a great deal to do with the accomplishments and interests of Charles, and it is a most fitting title to the building in a village that is so much in tune with nature.

25. THE WATER TOWER, FINEDON

At the western end of Finedon, beside the A6 road to Irthlingborough, stands this most elaborate Victorian tower. It is octagonal in shape and was constructed between 1903 and 1906 to supply Finedon and the local swimming bath with water. To the left of my illustration is the two-storey entrance porch which leads into the base of the tower. This has buttressing at each of the corners and the body of the tower is built in bands of contrasting coloured bricks. About two-thirds up the tower the walls are stepped out and within the decorated arcading are a series of windows, one on each face.

Until this elaborate construction was completed, the whole of Finedon's water supply came from either pumps or wells. The Urban District Council could not supply water until 1906, at which time the water tower must have been regarded as a symbol of significant progress to Finedon's residents.

The Victorian Water Tower, Finedon.

26. HINTON IN THE HEDGES

This view across the green at Hinton in the Hedges shows how well the combination of thatched cottages and stone houses with slate roofs blend with the more modern houses beyond.

Sir William Hinton held the manor here in 1346 and that, in part, is how the name of the village was derived. The other part is probably due to the fact that up until the end of the eighteenth century, the village lay on the main route from Brackley to Banbury. Later, a turnpike road was constructed and the village then became a backwater, deserving its cosy description of clipped hedges and thatched cottages – 'in the Hedges'.

Hinton in the hedges.

Just to the rear of the viewpoint of my illustration is the Church of the Holy Trinity, with its low tower built by the Normans. From this vantage point, eight heads on each side of the tower observe your approach. Traces of Saxon masonry suggest that today's church occupies the site of an earlier building of much simpler design.

In the past, English villages tended to develop around the church and such was the case in Hinton in the Hedges. The rectory was close by and adjacent to the village green and the almshouses built by Lord Crewe. In the past, many of the village residents depended on farming for their livelihood but today, as the residents tend to work outside the village, many of the farms and barns have been converted into modern dwellings.

Silver Street, Chacombe.

27. CHACOMBE

Situated about three miles from Banbury, amidst hills and woods, Chacombe is a quaint village almost on the border of Northamptonshire and Oxfordshire. During the mid-twelfth century, a priory of Augustinian canons was founded here by Hugh Chacombe, who served in Normandy as Henry II's justiciar, hence the name of the village.

Along the road to Banbury is the priory, with its medieval chapel and the remains of the former fish ponds nearby. At the foot of the hill, the house called Chacombe Priory is a handsome dwelling and was purchased by Michael Fox, a merchant in the city of London. The house was restored around 1600.

A short distance away is the Church of St Peter and St Paul, which dates from the thirteenth and fourteenth centuries, with much refurbishment during more recent times. A brass plate on the floor of the chancel commemorates Michael Fox of 1569. It carries the Arms of the Merchant Adventurers and the Arms of the City of London. He married twice and fathered seven children.

Many of the village properties were former business premises. Carefully restored, they are now attractive homes with names such as the 'Old Farmhouse' and the 'Old Forge'. About 400 years ago, the Bagley Bell Foundry was founded here and became the main suppliers of bells for churches and other establishments throughout this part of England. It is highly likely that Bell Cottage stands on the very site of this once-famous company.

About sixty years ago, Silver Street was the home to a number of working farms and a wheelwright's workshop. Today, Silver Street is well-known for its hostelry, the George and Dragon. From this viewpoint, the tower of the Church of St Peter and St Paul can be seen in the distance to the right.

East Carlton, Almshouses.

28. EAST CARLTON

A couple of miles to the west of Corby, just off the A427 road to Market Harborough, is East Carlton. In 1873, the Palmer family had their fine house built here in the style of a French chateau and it was set in beautiful parkland overlooking the Welland Valley. Today this extravagant looking house, with its huge iron gates, is visible from East Carlton Park.

The public park was created by the District Council and contains picnic areas, play areas and nature trails. Also here is the outcrop of the seam of ironstone which influenced the development of the huge iron and steel industry in this part of the county. The former coach house for the 'chateau' today houses a heritage centre and café.

Outside the gates of East Carlton Park, on Church Lane, stand these dignified old almshouses with high gables at each end. From the steeply pitched roof are four stout chimneys, and above the doorway in the centre of the building is the date 1668.

To the right of the almshouses is the Church of St Peter, which was rebuilt in 1788. It still retains its box pews, and within the South Chapel are a number of monuments to various members of the Palmer family.

Fawsley Hall.

29. FAWSLEY HALL

Fawsley Hall is indeed one of the most magnificent buildings in the county. It is situated about four miles to the south of Daventry and is surrounded by 2,000 acres of parkland. This superb old building was reopened in 1998 as a hotel.

At the time of Domesday a manor house, together with the primitive dwellings of peasant farmers, was situated here in 300 acres of land. By 1301, Simon de Daventre had bought the estate and assumed the name of 'de Fawsley'. By 1415, the estate had passed into the hands of the Knightley family, who were Puritans.

The quite outstanding architectural feature of the whole building is the two-storey bay window which has an enclosed balcony room which extends above the eaves of the roof. During the sixteenth century, access to this room was by way of a winding, narrow, external staircase. Tradition has it that it was in this room that the Puritan propaganda of the day was secretly printed under the supervision of Sir Richard Knightley.

Possibly the finest part of the house is the Great Hall, commissioned by Edmund Knightley in 1537. Its roof was removed in 1966 and reconstructed in 1988. Above the Tudor fireplace are the coats of arms of the Knightleys, Richard I and the twenty-six knights who travelled with him on the First Crusade.

By 1542, Edmund Knightley was knighted and became a commissioner for the Suppression of the Monasteries and the subsequent confiscation of the wealth and lands of the monasteries; thus the whole family enjoyed tremendous wealth. In 1575, Elizabeth I was entertained here in the south wing.

Much addition and development has gone on throughout the centuries at Fawsley Hall and today the visitor can reflect upon the many changes that have occurred in this fine old house.

The Wellington Tower, near Finedon.

30. THE WELLINGTON TOWER

Travellers along the A510 between Finedon and Thrapston will be familiar with this view of the building known as the Wellington Tower, or the Round House, which is situated just north of Finedon.

General Charles Arbuthnot, who resided at Woodford House, was a great friend of the Duke of Wellington and during one of the Duke's frequent visits to his home, the much-respected visitor mentioned to his host that there were certain similarities between the field where the Battle of Waterloo took place and the landscape in this part of Northamptonshire.

Following the Duke of Wellington's visit, the General had this unusual building completed with a plaque on the exterior wall incorporating the words: 'PANORAMA WATERLOO VICTORY JUNE 18 AD 1815'. A small platform, accessed by stairs from the first floor, affords the opportunity to view the surrounding countryside.

By the mid-nineteenth century, the building had become an inn. Later it was used as the private 'Waterloo Victory Social Club', which moved to other accommodation in 1895. Today this unusual building is a private residence.

St Botolph's Church, Slapton.

C. Holmes

31. SLAPTON CHURCH

Slapton is a small village standing, in part, on a low hill in the valley of the River Tove. Its narrow, twisting lanes contain some fine houses and cottages, many of which have been modified during recent years.

The village, whilst being attractive, is not dissimilar to others in this part of the county, but the reason why visitors come to Slapton is to visit the church. Dedicated to St Botolph, it stands alone on a grassy knoll with sheep grazing beside it and dates originally from the Norman period. The exterior appears to be of quite a basic design and so it is, as the design was changed and modified a great deal from the original by the builders during the Early English period. For instance, the base of the tower is Norman, the remainder is thirteenth century, with a window added 200 years later.

Inside this tiny church, the chancel being only 5ft wide by 10ft high, are the medieval wall paintings for which this church is famous. These fine examples of religious art date back approximately 600 years and were discovered about a century ago under a layer of lime wash. They must have been a glorious sight when first completed; St Francis of Assisi, St George and the dragon, St Nicholas and many more are here illuminating the walls of this simple, old building.

Bugbrooke.

32. BUGBROOKE

Buchebroc, as it was known at the time of Domesday, sits just to the south-west of Northampton, astride the B4525 road. The Grand Union Canal meanders through the village while the railway traffic, linking London and the north, speeds through at a faster pace. The River Nene flows to the north of the village, while one of its minor tributaries, Horse Stone Brook, gurgles restfully through the village.

Today it is a fairly quiet place, but 100 years or so ago it was quite a hive of activity. It had a number of bakeries, a mill, a brickyard and a number of tradespeople necessary to support everyday life. It also had one of the first soap factories in England. This connection with the past is now kept alive only by Heygates, the millers whose flour mills still flourish to the north of the village beside the River Nene. Few other industries from days of old have survived.

The church, dedicated to St Michael, is mainly of thirteenth- and fourteenth-century construction, but the four pointed arches in the south arcade point to Norman building techniques. Within the church is a quite remarkable rood screen dating from the fifteenth century, said to be one of the finest in the whole of Northamptonshire. The spire, atop its battlemented tower, gives the church a certain majestic appearance as it looks across the village from its raised vantage point.

Seen here is the junction of Great Lane, Ace Lane and the High Street.

33. BRIXWORTH CHURCH

The oldest church in England is St Martin's at Canterbury, but just a little younger is All Saints at Brixworth. In the days when Peterborough was called Medeshamstede and England was a colony of the Roman Empire, monks built this church at Brixworth.

Originally the church, the construction of which commenced about AD 675, was larger than the present building. The outer walls as we see them today were, centuries ago, a series of arcades, and an ambulatory with a vaulted roof was built around the walls of the chancel. It must have been a large building, for the historians tell us that in Saxon times the width of the church was 60ft.

When the Normans arrived they made numerous modifications to the building, including the blocking-up of the arches to form outer walls and the insertion of small windows within the arches. During medieval times, further changes were made, including the building of a chapel, the extending of the tower and the building of the spire above it.

Without doubt, the reason why we see so many red, tiled arches is because so much of the Roman building materials remained close to hand at the church's inception. The builders recovered thousands of Roman red tiles and they were used in the shaping of the chancel and the nave, and at every possible part of the building where an arch was to be constructed. This is emphasized particularly in the tranquil interior, where plain white walls give great contrast to those red Roman tiled arches.

The Church of All Saints at Brixworth is truly one of the most glorious pieces of ancient architecture in the county of Northamptonshire.

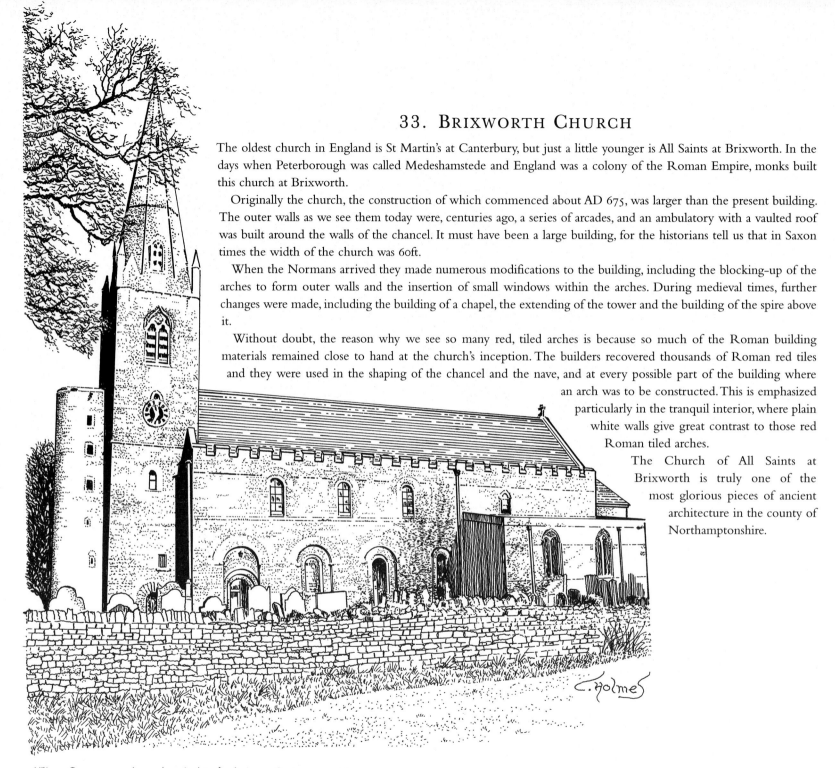

The Saxon church of All Saints, Brixworth.

The old Workhouse and the new Library, Brixworth.

34. BRIXWORTH WORKHOUSE

The village is dominated by its famous church upon the hill, while the remaining part of the former workhouse, constructed in 1837, stands close to more recent developments which surround it. It is an attractive building, with its protruding upper storey supported by stout columns. The design is similar to other workhouses constructed about the same time in other parts of the country. The building at Brixworth functioned for about 100 years and today is used as business premises. Next door to it stands the very modern library which has opened in recent years.

During the days of coach travel, the village became an important staging post for coaches travelling between London and the north of England. By 1851, the year of the Great Exhibition in London, the steam railway arrived at Brixworth and together with the development locally of iron ore deposits, the village changed from agricultural to industrial reliance. During this period many of the terraced, brick dwellings were built to house the workers and their families and new ale houses opened their doors to the new influx of customers.

Today the village is surrounded by the manmade grassy hills and hollows, the scars left after the ironstone workings ran out.

The old village shop, the memorial and the village green, Culworth.

35. CULWORTH

Culworth is a quiet and attractive village where a former village shop, pretty cottages and the war memorial look out over a large green. In days gone by, the local cattle and produce were auctioned here on market days. It is thought that a Stone Age settlement existed nearby and that the mound close to the church known as Berry Hill is all that remains of a fortified dwelling constructed during the dark days of the reign of King Stephen.

The church, dedicated to St Mary, dates from the twelfth century; it has an intricately-carved Jacobean pulpit and some interesting stone corbels, although much of the building is Victorian.

For about a ten-year period during the late eighteenth century, Culworth and the surrounding villages were terrorised by a group of thugs. These burglars and highwaymen, numbering about a dozen, attacked stage coaches, robbed travellers and broke into houses. This was not only locally, but it was said that they also operated in Warwickshire, Buckinghamshire and Oxfordshire. Strangely, the parish clerk of the not too distant Sulgrave was said to be a gang member. He was a shoemaker by trade, and rumour had it that he carried a pair of pistols and hid the gang's booty in Sulgrave Church. In 1787, the Culworth Gang were ambushed at Blakesley and after being tried at Towcester Assizes, peace returned to this part of the county.

Aldwincle.

36. ALDWINCLE

Where the River Nene makes a big curve between the villages of Wadenhoe and Thorpe Waterville lies Aldwincle. The Saxons referred to this place as 'Wincel' meaning 'where the river bends' and it easy therefore to see where part of the name for today's village came from. The village consists of a pleasant mixture of red brick and grey stone houses. Some still have thatched roofs, while others sit beneath a roof of slate or pantile.

In 1631, John Dryden, playwright and poet, was born at the rectory, more recently known as Dryden House, which is situated just across the road from the now-redundant Church of All Saints. During the late seventeenth century, he gained a reputation of being the best living English poet. Both his parents came from titled families who were Puritan in religion and politics. The young Dryden paid tribute to Cromwell in his first poem of note, but when Charles II came to the throne Dryden welcomed him also.

In April 2009, a painting of John Dryden, the first Poet Laureate, went on show at the National Portrait Gallery. It was believed to have been painted in 1668 by M.J. Wright, Charles II's court artist, and was purchased by the gallery for £225,000.

This view of Aldwincle shows the other church, St Peter's. It has one of the most graceful spires in Northamptonshire rising from a fourteenth-century tower. The attractive, old Village Hall is to the left. How nice to see the very modern climbing frames and slides, provided for the local children, in between these two elegant structures.

Locally it is said that there was, in days gone by, a local carrier who used to hire out horses, rather like today's hire car companies. His name was Tommy Hobson and he gave no choice of horse to those who used his stable, for the animal they got was always the one nearest to the door. Hence today's saying of 'Hobson's choice'. In fact, it was no choice at all!

Barby.

37. BARBY

Situated at almost 500ft above sea level and close to Daventry and Rugby, the village of Barby overlooks the plains of Warwickshire to the north and west. Just to the north of the village, evidence has been found of a Roman settlement and at Castle Mound, there once stood a medieval castle.

In 1832, the story *Tom Brown's Schooldays* was published, and in it, the Barby Run is mentioned. During more recent years, the runners from Rugby School were no longer required to circle the church at Barby, as in the book, but just to return from Barby to Rugby.

Over the centuries the main means of employment was in agriculture but, during the eighteenth century, weaving also became important. By 1950, many people had left the village to seek work in the nearby towns, but during the 1960s many new houses where constructed here and the dwindling population was replenished.

The village consists of a mixture of dwellings, the earliest being about 400 years old. A few houses are cob built, but Northamptonshire stone and brick are much in evidence. No doubt in years gone by much of the village was thatched, but there is little evidence of that today.

This view in Kilsby Road caught my eye; Boseworth Cottage with its buttressing is on the left, and facing it across the road is Walnut Cottage with a corrugated iron roof.

Finally, there should be a mention of the village's ghost story. Back in 1851, Mrs Webb, a village resident, died and left all her worldly goods, including her cottage, to her nephew. He let the cottage to a family who were woken on a number of occasions by an old woman (presumably the ghost of Mrs Webb) who pointed upwards to a trapdoor in the ceiling. After being informed of this, her nephew went into the loft and discovered a bag of gold coins and certain papers detailing the old lady's debts. After he had paid off the debts, the ghost was never seen again.

38. WEEKLEY POST OFFICE

The main road linking Oxford to Stamford, the A43, passes close to Weekley, which is situated just to the north of Kettering and near to Boughton House. The village is certainly an attractive one, with numerous old stone buildings, some still beneath thatched roofs. In Church Walk, the village school was opened in 1624 by Nicholas Latham, and just opposite is the eighteenth-century Village Hall.

Most of the church dates from the thirteenth to the fifteenth century, but the attractive south doorway is unmistakably Norman. The Montagu family, the original owners of Boughton House, are well represented in the church since over the generations they contributed generously to the upkeep of the building. Sir Edward was the Chief Justice during the sixteenth century and a fine alabaster painted figure commemorates his death in 1557.

For me, the image of Weekley is that seen by today's traveller, the view of the thatched cottages and the fine stone buildings beyond. If there should ever be a contest for the prettiest Post Office in the county, I feel that the Post Office at Weekley would surely be a great contender.

The Post Office and cottages, Weekley.

C. Holmes

Weekley.

39. THE MONTAGU HOSPITAL, WEEKLEY

Shown here is the old hospital with the war memorial and the Church of St Mary at Weekley. It was designed to accommodate seven poor, old men with two women to attend to them, and was founded by Edward Montagu in 1611. Now a private house, this handsome stone building stands between the church and the school and is adorned with small obelisks and carved gables. The motto of Edward Montagu reads, 'What thou doest, do it in faith', and above the door a message in Latin warns us that life is short and time goes by us as we grow old with the silent years.

Triangular Lodge, Rushton.

40. THE TRIANGULAR LODGE, RUSHTON

Regarded by many as one of the most strange and curious buildings ever devised, it sits beside a minor road to Rushton, just a couple of miles outside Desborough. It is one of Sir Thomas Tresham's almost fanatical declarations of his faith.

On his release from a thirteen-year prison sentence for his Catholic beliefs, he devised this three-sided creation in 1593, thereby adding one of many examples of his strange architectural concepts to the landscape of Northamptonshire. The Triangular Lodge was his way of symbolising the Holy Trinity. Its design is based on an equilateral triangle and has three sides, three floors and three windows on each floor and on each side. On each side are three gables, with three pinnacles and a 33ft long frieze; also on each side are thirty-three letters.

Initially this folly was intended as a keeper's lodge for the Rushton Hall estate and while the interior is quite simple, the exterior is very ornate. The translations from the lettering on the north side roughly mean, 'Who shall separate us from the love of Christ', on the south-east side, 'Let the Earth open and bring forth a Saviour' and on the south-west side, 'I have considered thy works, O Lord, and have been afraid'.

Grafton Underwood.

41. GRAFTON UNDERWOOD

The tiny tributary of the River Nene, the Alledge Brook, complete with ducks, flows beneath a series of four bridges beside the main street of Grafton Underwood. A broad verge lies on the western side of the river, which is overlooked on both sides by seventeenth- and eighteenth-century cottages in a pale, honey-coloured limestone, most of them with thatched roofs; the scene is almost Cotswolds-like. The manor house, now the rectory, dates from the 1653 and the former village pub, the Dukes Arms, from 1652. The school was constructed during the mid-1800s by the then Duke of Buccleuch, whose successors in the title owned the village until recent years.

The Church of St James is interesting and varied, being composed of a mixture of architectural styles. The nave and the tower are the oldest, both being Norman. In 1757, a boy was born locally and he lived for sixty-eight years. During his lifetime, he became a schoolmaster and a parish clerk. The remarkable thing is that he had no hands but learnt to write holding a pen in his mouth. A sample of his work is kept in the church. A more recent addition to St James's is the stained glass window dedicated to the members of the American Eighth Airforce who lost their lives during the Second World War and who were stationed nearby.

42. JESUS HOSPITAL, ROTHWELL

Back in 1154, Rothwell had a market and, by 1204, King John had granted permission for an annual fair to take place the week after Trinity Sunday. The market square is dominated by the Church of the Holy Trinity. This is the longest church in Northamptonshire and dates back to Norman times. To the south-east of the church stands Jesus Hospital, an Elizabethan almshouse.

Jesus Hospital was founded in 1591 by Owen Ragsdale, who was a fellow of Magdalen College, Oxford, and a Grammar School teacher. In 1551, he became a chorister at Magdalen College and by 1560, he held a BA degree. He inherited a huge amount of land in Yorkshire and became extremely rich. In 1582, he endowed the Rothwell Grammar School where he had previously taught. His foundation for the Jesus Hospital was for twenty-six old men, with a room for each widower situated around the courtyard. Additionally, there were four halls where they could all meet together.

The entrance is through this lovely old gateway, with its finely carved stonework and elaborate top. The lettering carved into the stonework above the arch is still clearly legible after all these centuries and beyond the gateway the attractive courtyard can be seen.

Much restoration to the whole complex has been carried out since its inception, the most recent being in 1962. Today, with the addition of central heating and accommodation for married couples, this lovely old building is still in use.

Jesus Hospital Gateway, Rothwell.

Grafton Regis.

43. GRAFTON REGIS

Almost midway between Milton Keynes and Northampton, Grafton Regis sits on a hill beside the busy A508 road. The scene I have chosen to illustrate shows the view that most motorists who travel this route will be familiar with; the old pub, the White Hart, together with its attendant cottages.

To the east of the road, the rest of the old village drifts toward the Grand Union Canal and consists of little more than the old rectory, the former school, the church and various farm buildings. However this tiny, apparently insignificant, hamlet has a place in English history, for it was here where Edward IV met Elizabeth Woodville, whom he married in 1464. Their unfortunate offspring were the 'Princes in the Tower'. During later years, Richard III stayed at the manor and Henry VIII enjoyed the company of Ann Boleyn here so much so that he bestowed on the village the title 'Regis'.

Following the English Civil War, when Charles II regained the throne, he conferred the Dukedom of Grafton on his son, Henry FitzRoy, in 1675. Over the centuries, the Woodvilles and the FitzRoys have been prominent in the history of the county.

The Church of St Mary's has many memorials and monuments to the families of the Woodvilles and the FitzRoys alike. The church was constructed during the twelfth and fourteenth centuries, the tower being built by Sir John Woodville early in the fifteenth century. It retains a scratch dial close to the small doorway into the belfry from a time long before clocks were invented. Fine views across the surrounding landscape to the canal beyond may be enjoyed from outside the church, which is perched on its own piece of high ground.

Walgrave.

44. WALGRAVE

This is the view of Walgrave from the Kettering Road, the town of Kettering being about six miles away. To the left, standing on elevated ground, is the Church of St Peter's and the brick building, on the extreme right, was formerly an inn called the Travellers Rest Inn, dated 1877.

Formerly a Saxon settlement, the village was later mentioned in the Domesday Book and today it is a large village of old stone cottages, some Victorian terraced houses, a mix of council houses and some fine modern homes. On the High Street the former Co-op is now a private residence, but the small Post Office and store is still open for business. On the south-eastern edge of the village is Hall Farm, all that remains of a large house, parts of which date from Elizabethan times.

During the reign of James I, John Williams, the rector at Walgrave, was chosen to become Chaplain to the King. Gradually, and by unworthy methods, he worked his way up to becoming Archbishop of York before eventually being replaced by Archbishop Laud. However, for a village in a county that supported the Parliamentarian cause, perhaps the best claim to fame that Walgrave has is that Cromwell's boots are said to have been made here.

The 14th. century bridge, Irthlingborough.

45. IRTHLINGBOROUGH

Artleborough, as the town was known in times gone by, was frequently referred to as 'a large village with industry'. In those days, due to the generous local ironstone deposits, blast furnaces operated day and night providing work for the surrounding population. During later years, Irthlingborough relied on the production of footwear for its livelihood. Today it is probably known for its football club, Rushden and Diamonds, and for the Nene Park complex.

Just off the A45, a short distance from Wellingborough and close to the River Nene, is the Church of St Peter, built on the site as a Norman church in about 1354. There is evidence that a thirteenth-century church also stood on the same site.

At the centre of the town is the main street, about a mile in length, bordered by picturesque old buildings. Looking down from the top of eight stone steps is the medieval column of the market cross with its foliage and ballflower ornamentation.

The town has two fine bridges to cross the broad waters of the River Nene here. The twentieth-century bridge, built out of necessity to accommodate modern traffic, is functional rather than impressive and runs alongside the older bridge, which is a most attractive piece of architecture. It was constructed during the fourteenth century and has ten ribbed arches. The monastic arms, the 'cross keys' carved on one of its stones, suggests that it was built by monks of Peterborough. The bridge was restored in 1925.

The Town Hall in Bridge Street, Brackley.

46. BRACKLEY

Brackley is a small and pleasant town set amongst the attractive countryside of the south-west of the county. At the southern end of its main thoroughfare, Bridge Street, stands the handsome Town Hall, which was originally built on arches in 1706 to provide a small, covered market space at road level. By 1884 the lower storey was enclosed and it was used as the corn market. Today's markets are held every Friday in the Market Place, beyond which the broad, tree-lined street becomes the High Street and stretches for over a mile into Northampton Road.

It is said that Bracca, who came from Halse and lived sometime between AD 550 and AD 650, built a village in a clearing and called it Braccaley, which has evolved into today's name of Brackley. Both Roman and Iron Age remains have been found locally, but the town probably expanded more during the Norman period, and by the thirteenth century it was important enough to have representatives at trade meetings in London. During this time, its castle was built, but little remains today in Hinton Road. In 1215, the year of the Magna Carta, and again in 1264, the King met the barons here, thus the town has early connections with the establishment of English freedom.

In 1150 the Hospital of St James and St John was founded on the eastern side of the High Street, passing during later years to Magdalen College, Oxford. During the Dissolution of the Monasteries, the Grammar School was founded and is still in existence today, while the old hospital chapel, much refurbished during the late 1800s, is still standing.

Just to the left of my illustration is the Crown Hotel, a leftover from the time when Brackley was an important coaching town and boasted no less than twenty-eight inns. During the fire of 1649, the Crown Inn was damaged, but it seems not as badly as some of the surrounding buildings, probably due to their thatched roofs. Today it has an eighteenth-century front and looks to be of a sturdy construction as it sits well amidst the other buildings of Brackley's centre.

The Crewe Almshouses, Brackley.

47. THE CREWE ALMSHOUSES, BRACKLEY

This dignified old terrace of houses stands on the right-hand side of the junction of High Street and Church Road when entering Brackley along the Northampton Road. The almshouses were founded in 1633 by Sir Thomas Crewe, who later became Lord Crewe of Steane. During the English Civil War, he was an enthusiastic supporter of the Parliamentary cause for he was a dedicated Puritan. Following the closure of the Hospital of St James and St John at Brackley, there was no accommodation available for the poor and although small in size, these almshouses went some way to remedy this problem. These fine, old stone houses, with their stone mullion windows, have two storeys with dormers in the roof. In 1969, they were refurbished and modified in order to provide accommodation in four flats.

48. MOULTON

About four miles to the north of the county town, and surrounded by vast housing estates and industrial developments, the old village centre of Moulton, a conservation area, still retains a certain old world charm. On Stocks Hill, where in recent years the stocks have been returned, the local Morris dancers entertain the village residents each Boxing Day.

The name Moulton is synonymous with one of the village's most famous residents, William Carey. Carey came from Paulersbury and settled in Moulton in 1785. He started a school, which he must have found very difficult to maintain on his humble income, and he was also a preacher and a shoemaker. His congregation paid him 4s a week and erected a chapel for him. An additional collection resulted in sufficient contributions to pay for a black suit for him to preach in. His financial position improved a little when he met Thomas Gotch of Kettering, who supplied him with plenty of shoes to repair and 10s a week to encourage him to continue to read and improve his education. This he did, and in 1792 Carey founded the Baptist Missionary Society; a year later he became a missionary in India, where he died in 1834. The chapel was extended in 1870 and close by, the William Carey Memorial Hall was built in 1958. These building are just to the left of my illustration, which shows the Carey cottage and the Telegraph restaurant, with the fine building of the Northamptonshire College of Agriculture, built in 1913, beyond.

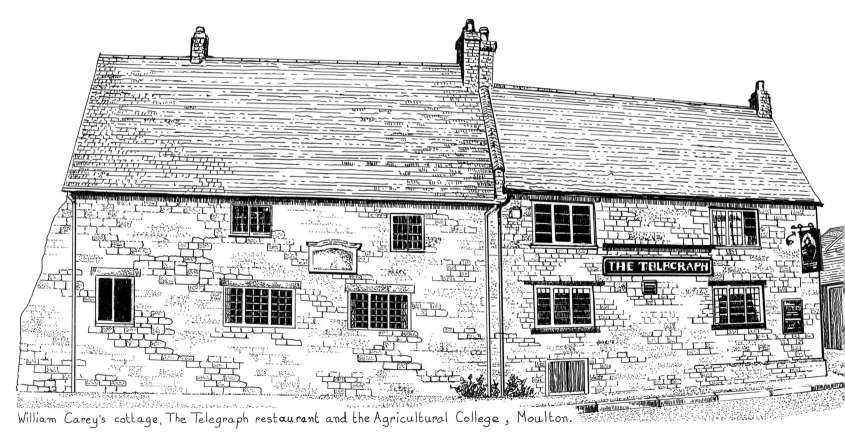

William Carey's cottage, The Telegraph restaurant and the Agricultural College, Moulton.

Church Street, Moulton.

The view down Moulton's Church Street is shown at the top of the page, the battlemented tower of the church being visible from some distance away as the village stands on high ground. A fragment of a Saxon cross was found in years gone by beneath the foundations of the nave of the Church of St Peter and St Paul. The present church is of medieval construction and was commenced in 1298, replacing an earlier church which was ruined in 1265 during the Barons War. This fine ironstone building contains three main doorways, dating from the fourteenth century, and in the nave are four round arches with a fragment of window above, all from the Norman period.

Finally it is little-known that the world famous disinfectant Jeyes Fluid was developed by Philadelphus and John Jeyes, the chemists from Moulton.

Kettering Railway Station.

49. KETTERING RAILWAY STATION

For many of those who use Kettering Railway Station, particularly those of tender years, it is probably just a place where one gets on and off the train, but to me it is a reminder of what railway stations used to be like, a reminder of the architecture and craftsmanship of an age long since past.

The railway through Kettering was part of the extension of the Midland Railway connecting Hitchin, in Hertfordshire, with Northampton and Huntingdon. In the initial stages it was felt that the railway would provide an economical method of transport for coal, coke and ironstone, not to mention passengers. The line was opened with great ceremony and celebration in May 1857. The station was designed by C.H. Driver and built by Edwin Brown of Wellingborough. The design is of a more or less standard layout for its time, but the structure as a whole is remarkable for its fine ironwork, and the 'pieced grill' casting is claimed to be amongst the finest examples left in England.

During the 1970s, British Rail had threatened to demolish parts of these old structures as correct maintenance was proving to be a problem, particularly the glasswork in the overhead canopies. Following discussions with the Kettering Civic Society, British Rail decided that preservation work was to be carried out on the ironwork, the platform canopies and the station buildings. Since then, an almost continuous programme of refurbishment has taken place on the station itself; flood lighting at the station front has been added, trees have been planted and the car park improved. It has been a highly commendable effort by all concerned.

This is Platform 2a, with ironwork and platform canopies. The detail shown, top right, gives an indication of the intricacy of the canopy supports.

50. OLD

A mile or so to the east of Lamport and north of Pitsford Reservoir is the village of Old. At the time of Domesday it was called Walda, which later became Wold, which without the 'W' gives today's name of Old.

Within the village there are a number of fine stone buildings dating from the seventeenth century; the brewery house, the manor house and the old rectory being examples. As a contrast there are a number of more recently constructed brick buildings. Just as in many other villages throughout the land, Old had its own butcher, smithy and bakehouse to serve the needs of the residents, but most of these former business premises have long since been converted into comfortable homes.

The village still has its pub, the White Horse, which stands facing the Harrington Road and the lime tree planted in 1887 to mark Queen Victoria's Golden Jubilee. Beside the pub runs a track which gives access to Grange Farm and to the vast Church of St Andrew.

From this track the imposing Perpendicular church tower is seen to the right, while to the left are the buildings that at one time housed the village school and the school house.

The church dates from the late thirteenth century but was extensively restored during the late nineteenth century. Inside the roof of the nave, the carvings represent the twelve apostles; close by the north door are further carvings, while the bench ends in the choir stalls also carry examples. A church of this size certainly indicates that here, in the past, was a wealthy community.

Old.

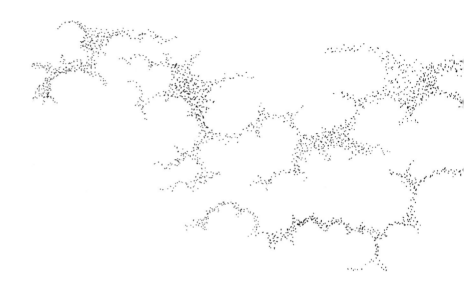

51. Isham

Almost midway between Wellingborough and Kettering, the village of Isham sits astride the A509. Before the days when huge vehicles choked our roads and everyone drove a car, and the railways carried most of the freight and passengers, Isham had two railway stations on the Leicester-Hitchin Midland Railway. Today they have long since ceased to function and, in spite of the traffic on the main road, the village is a very pleasant place.

I could not resist this view of the beautiful thatched cottage with the twelfth-century Church of St Peter beyond and the houses across the main road as seen from Middle Street. High upon the tower of the majestic-looking church is a frieze of panelling just below the battlements, and at each corner is a ferocious looking monster, each watching over a different aspect of village life. Although most of the building dates from the twelfth century, many architectural periods are represented, including Norman and Early English. On one of the Norman capitols in the nave, for instance, are four small heads with sprays of foliage issuing from their mouths. The pulpit is Jacobean and the candleholder, situated near the altar, holds fourteen candles and dates from shortly after the Battle of Waterloo. The altar rail is from the seventeenth century.

The village consists of a mixture of traditional limestone cottages, some still thatched, and a number of modern houses. Down by the River Ise there used to be a mill. During its lifetime it had various uses, and during the late 1700s it was a paper mill.

Middle Street and St Peter's, Isham.

71

52. PAULERSPURY

Paulerspury lies in the south-east of the county. I have chosen to illustrate the old school building for two reasons. The first must be for its most unusual design; I have never before seen such an elaborate clock tower on a primary school. It was constructed in 1861 and has a delightful carving of children reading books. The clock itself has been placed on stone columns and above it is a tower with a high pinnacle. It is indeed a most unusual piece of Gothic architecture. The second reason is that this school stands on the site of the earlier school where Edmund Carey, father of William Carey, taught for fifty years. Just to the left of my illustration is the Vine House Hotel.

The cottage where William Carey was born has long since gone, but Carey's Row in Paulerspury is where it stood. The family had resided in the village for generations and William's grandfather was the first schoolmaster in the village. At the age of fourteen, the boy was sent to Piddington to become a cobbler. This he did, but he longed to travel to foreign lands and spread the gospel. As he grew older and his beliefs became stronger, he combined his shoemaking skills with his ability as a preacher and ultimately in 1793, he left for India and the life of a missionary. He died forty years later. A tablet just inside the porch of the Church of St James at Paulerspury reminds us of this great man's work.

During the thirteenth and fourteenth centuries, the Lords of the Manor in this part of Northamptonshire were a family with the name of Parueli and the village derives its name of Paruelos-Puri from that family. The Romans were here even earlier and it was at that time noted for the production of fruit from its orchards. From the time of Henry VIII to the time of Elizabeth I, the Throgmorton family resided locally and a daughter of the family, Bess Throgmorton, became the wife of Sir Walter Raleigh. During the Victorian period, the village became well-known for the high quality of its lace; perhaps the best-known lacemaker was a Mrs Dunkerly, who produced lace for Queen Victoria.

Paulerspury.

53. BECKET'S WELL, NORTHAMPTON

Back in 1164, Thomas a Becket, Archbishop of Canterbury, had refused to conform to the demand of Henry II that all church courts should be brought under the control of the King.

He was imprisoned in the great castle of Northampton because of his refusal but somehow he managed to escape his captors and, disguised as a humble monk, he was able to take refuge at the priory of Hannington, a few miles to the north. Further legends tell of him being given refuge for a time at a mill along the banks of the River Nene before he made good his escape to France. During his flight from Northampton, he is said to have stopped to take a sip of water at a spring on the south side of Northampton and over the centuries the place has become known as Becket's Well.

Thomas a Becket was martyred in Canterbury Cathedral in 1170 and canonized in 1172. The place where he is reputed to have taken refreshment at Northampton was marked, in true Victorian style, by the construction of a fine Gothic-style well-house in 1843. He is also commemorated in the name of the nearby park, at least one public house, a school and his image at the Guild Hall.

This is Becket's Well as it is today beside the A428 road to Bedford.

Becket's Well.

C. Holmes

73

The Guildhall, Northampton.

54. THE GUILDHALL, NORTHAMPTON

Northampton's Guildhall stands majestically in St Giles Street, a monument to Victorian overindulgence and intricate decoration. It is, I think, the most elaborate building in the county, with a front almost as detailed as a cathedral.

The east side was designed by E.W. Godwin and completed in 1864; the west side being the work of A.W. Jeffrey and M.H. Holding and added in 1892. This ornate two-storey building was so well designed that it gives the impression of being built at the same time.

One of the main aims of the designers must have been to convey to the public the vast wealth of connections that the town and the county has had with persons both famous and important to the history of England and to certain events that had influenced the shaping and development of this country. As a result, there are numerous stone effigies that decorate the stonework including Edward I, Queen Eleanor, Richard I, the poet Dryden, Queen Victoria, Henry VI, Thomas a Becket and the Battle of Naseby.

Inside are wall and ceiling decorations which continue this theme. Included are Richard II, Lawrence Washington, Charles I, William Carey and Oliver Cromwell, to mention but a few. The Guildhall is truly a fine building and an example of the exuberance of Victorian excesses.

To the right stand the much simpler, more recently designed Northampton Borough Council offices. It is a dignified building that fits in well beside its older companion.

Abington Park Museum, Northampton.

C. Holmes

55. ABINGTON PARK MUSEUM, NORTHAMPTON

A familiar sight to most of the town's residents is the former manor house in Abington Park. Standing in vast parkland, the building that today houses a fine museum was in times past the manor house in the village of Abington. The Church of St Peter and St Paul stands close to the house and together they were part of the scene that must have been familiar to the granddaughter of William Shakespeare when she moved here with her second husband, John Barnard.

Her husband had an estate here and was knighted by Charles II in 1661. Unfortunately the marriage was a childless union and although she inherited many of the books and manuscripts of the poet, little is known today of their whereabouts. In the will of Sir John Barnard, the books were believed to be valued at less than £30. Elizabeth is only mentioned as an afterthought on the gravestone of Sir John Barnard in the South Chapel of the church.

Their fine house, however, still stands and dates mainly from the seventeenth and eighteenth centuries, but parts of the building are Tudor in origin. The Oak Room and hallway with its hammer beam roof are both handsome. There are numerous rooms to visit, with many paintings and relics from Naseby's battlefield, and also prints and posters and a separate section for the regiments of Northamptonshire. It is a fine building with fine contents.

56. ST PETER'S CHURCH, NORTHAMPTON

Said to be one of the finest Norman churches in England, St Peter's in Northampton was initially constructed during the twelfth century. The tower has attractive horizontal lines of limestone, sandstone and ironstone. Even today, the contrast between light and dark stonework is quite remarkable and the circular buttressing on the tower is almost unique. The tower is capped by a squat, pyramidal-shaped roof which is not visible from this ground level viewpoint.

The construction of the church was commenced about 100 years after the Norman Conquest by Simon de St Liz, the first Norman Earl of Northampton. During this period, following the subjugation of the Saxon people, the Normans became involved in a huge building programme, developing cathedrals and churches throughout the land.

Excavations close to St Peter's have revealed that before 1066 it was the site of an early Saxon settlement dated between AD 400 and AD 650 and it is felt that this was the original Hamtun settlement, a royal estate which by AD 900 developed into an important Danish town.

St Peter's has been described as a remarkable spectacle of Norman arcading due to the numerous arches which adorn its walls. The builders have indeed produced an interior of tremendous visual impact, with decorative arcading on the arches and fine pier carvings in the nave. A mixture of carved heads, flying creatures, foliage and animals adorn the capitals of the columns, while the entrance into the tower is beneath a well-decorated Norman arch.

Truly St Peter's is a remarkable building and an outstanding example of the work of the craftsmen of long ago.

St Peter's Church, Northampton.

Wood Cottage, the Old Post Office with the Kings Head beyond, Apethorpe.

57. APETHORPE

A tiny tributary of the River Nene, the Willow Brook flows through the village and, in true English style, it glides beneath a small, humpbacked bridge and close by a group of old stone cottages.

The picturesque village of Apethorpe, mentioned in the Domesday Book, was once inside the vast forests of Rockingham. It was the Romans who first constructed dwellings close to the river bank and beside the old Roman road, Ermine Street, as it continued toward Stamford.

Situated between Woodnewton and Kings Cliffe, the village consists of stone-built houses beneath thatched, tiled and Collyweston slate roofs. Originally all part of the estate belonging to the manor, the village houses still retain their former business titles, such as Dairy Cottage and Laundry Cottage. Here is Wood Cottage, the old Post Office, with the village pub just beyond. The Kings Head was built around the end of the nineteenth century on the site of a much earlier establishment. Close to the manor house, a group of fine houses have recently been completed, while closer to the church the former village school of 1846 is now a private dwelling.

Apethorpe Hall was built by Sir Walter Mildmay during the sixteenth century. He was Lord of the Manor here and, like many others of his time, he became extremely rich as a result of him being in the right place at the right time during Henry VIII's Dissolution of the Monasteries. He founded Emmanuel College at Cambridge and, as you would expect, his family is well represented in the church. Within St Leonard's they have their own chapel inside, dated 1621, which is the rather pompous looking Mildmay monument in black marble. The east window of the chapel is particularly attractive and 'the Last Supper' in the chancel window dates from the eighteenth century and is considered to be something of a rarity.

The embattled tower of the church was constructed in 1633 and a pyramidal-shaped steeple rises above it. The church itself is mainly of Perpendicular design, consisting of nave, side aisles and chancel.

Cold Ashby.

58. COLD ASHBY

At the very centre of the village and standing on high ground, the Church of St Denis dominates the surrounding cottages. It is approached by a most elaborate stone lych-gate, dated 1883, which is not visible from this viewpoint. It is thought that the carved stonework in the vestry dates from the Saxon period and that the north doorway is Norman. The remainder of the church, with the exception of the fifteenth-century tower, was constructed between 1200 and 1300. One of its bells dates from 1317, making it one of the oldest in the land.

Cold Ashby stands in the north-west of the county, straddling the main road from Market Harborough to Daventry, and is the highest village in Northamptonshire at almost 700ft above sea level. The 'Cold' part of the name dates from a time when we had cold winters and, due to its position, it was said that snow always lingered here for weeks after it had cleared from other parts of the county.

A mile or so from the village is Honey Hill, from where there are fine views in good weather across the nearby counties of Leicestershire and Warwickshire.

Back in 1550, Richard Knolles was born at Cold Ashby. He became famous in his day as a writer. He wrote *History of the Turks*, which was well thought of by Dr Johnson and Lord Bryon, who said that Knolles was one of the finest writers whose works he enjoyed as a child.

Thorpe Manderville Manor.

59. THORPE MANDEVILLE

The village of Torp, as it was called at the time of Domesday, lies on the eastern slope of a hill in southern Northamptonshire. Culworth is close by and the border of Oxfordshire is just a short distance away. It was originally a Danish settlement, perhaps one of the earliest in the county. During the thirteenth century, Richard Amundeville was Lord of the Manor, hence today's name of Thorpe Mandeville.

The village church is dedicated to St John the Baptist and dates from the fourteenth century, although a church was in existence here as early as 1163. The short saddleback tower, with its depiction of St John on its east wall, has a plain parapet with gargoyles and crocketted pinnacles at its four corners.

Inside the church are a number of memorials, one of which in the north aisle is to the memory of the Kirton family, who were related to Oliver Cromwell. Also here are three wall paintings thought to date from the fourteenth and fifteenth centuries.

Thorpe Mandeville still retains a number of old stone buildings. The finest of these is the former rectory, now over 400 years old, which later became known as the Court. Dove Cottages are much humbler dwellings, although nevertheless appealing in appearance, while the attractive Ivy Cottage was the home of the village shoemaker in days gone by.

Seen here is the 'new' manor house as viewed on a winter's day from the churchyard. This handsome stone structure was built by a niece of Oliver Cromwell some time after the English Civil War. The earlier manor house, having been garrisoned by Parliamentary troops during those troubled times, no longer exists.

The old village pub, the Three Connies, has on one of its walls a sundial with the dates 1622 and 1847 on it. In former times it became the meeting place for the Bicester Hounds and until the mid-1800s, the local magistrates met here too. It developed as an inn, providing accommodation for the cattle drovers on the route known as Banbury Lane.

60. NETHER HEYFORD

At the junction of Weedon Road and Church Street in Nether Heyford, the village war memorial stands on a tiny green close to this beautiful oak tree.

Just across Weedon Road is the huge five-acre green, on which many village functions have been held. Until 1924 the right to graze livestock here was much sought after. It is difficult to imagine how busy the village must have been in times gone by, for until 1891 three blast furnaces operated here producing iron from local ironstone, the name Furnace Lane being a reminder of those days of industry in the village.

Close to the Grand Union Canal, and to the west of Northampton, the village was known as Heiforde at the time of Domesday. The village has expanded greatly during the last forty years or so, perhaps due to its close proximity to the M1 motorway.

In the past the village had a 'good guy' and a 'bad guy'. The local rogue was Francis Morgan, who was the Judge of the King's Bench and it was he who pronounced the sentence of death on Lady Jane Grey. He was said to have taken his own life in 1556. Full of remorse, he lamented, 'Take away the Lady Jane from me'.

A more popular figure came much later. He was a local wine merchant by the name of William Bliss who bequeathed the sum of £400 in 1674 to build and maintain a school overlooking the main green. It was opened in 1683 and rebuilt in true Victorian style in 1880.

The Church of St Peter and St Paul dates mainly from the thirteenth and fourteenth centuries. The chancel and the tower have carved heads around them, while much carving in the form of shields, angels and heads abounds within the building. Inside the chancel, a fine brass portrait depicts Sir Walter Mauntell and his wife holding hands. He was a knight who fought in the War of the Roses and died in 1467. In the south aisle is a finely-detailed alabaster monument of the 'bad guy', Sir Francis Morgan.

The junction of Weedon Road and Church Steet, Nether Hayford.

61. ABTHORPE

At Towcester, the little river that gurgles by is known as the River Tove, but about three miles to the south west it is called the River Sow, beside which sits Abthorpe.

Most of the village was owned by the Duke of Grafton until as recently as the 1920s, the links with the family reaching back into history. For many years the Grafton Hunt would meet on the village green, and during the late 1800s a considerable contribution was made by the Grafton family to help the restoration of the Church of St John the Baptist.

With its tower at its northern end, the church is of unusual layout and is in fact a recent version of the Early English and Decorated styles. Prior to 1736 it was a chapelry which was dependant upon the vicarage of Towcester. Today's church replaced the earlier church and was built by Ewan Christian in 1871, using money left to the village by Jane Leeson and John Nicholl.

Facing the church, at the opposite end of the village green, is the old village school built in 1642 as a free school by the same Jane Leeson.

Shown here is the main street with the Church of St John the Baptist beyond. Many of the old business premises within the village have been converted to private dwellings, but in the past shoemaking and lacemaking kept many of the residents employed.

Main Street, Abthorpe.

Prebendal Manor House, Nassington.

84

62. NASSINGTON

To the north of Fotheringhay and close to the western border of Cambridgeshire is Nassington, a large village which has a number of attractive parts. It has much for the visitor to admire in the groups of stone cottages and houses, with a variety of architectural styles dating from various periods in history up to the present day. The main reason for me coming here, however, was to visit the oldest house in the county and the longest continually inhabited in England, the Prebendal Manor.

With the close proximity of the River Nene, Nassington became an ideal place for people to settle. This was proved in 1942 when an Anglo-Saxon cemetery was uncovered, revealing fifty graves and artefacts from that period. In the Church of St Mary's and All Saints there is evidence of Saxon work, not least of all in the nave, and the church's oldest possession is part of a carved Saxon cross. Much of the earlier church was rebuilt during the thirteenth and fifteenth centuries, and during the latter period an octagonal tower and spire were set atop the earlier squared tower.

It is said that shortly after 1017, King Cnut (Canute) visited his royal manor at Nassington. Enlarged after this period, it would have then been a timber building with a roof of thatch. By 1123, the manor and its lands were owned by the Bishop of Lincoln to provide a prebend for the canons of Lincoln. The prebend was an estate belonging to the church at Nassington which provided an income to Lincoln.

Much modified over the centuries, the property was sold in 1875 by the Ecclesiastical Commission to the Earl of Carysfoot, who rented it out to tenant farmers. Derelict by 1968, it was purchased by the present owner when a period of renovation commenced.

The rear of the present building is shown here, with the church to the left, while to the far left is the 24ft square dovecote which provided nests for 700 pairs of birds.

The Watch Tower, Pilton.

63. PILTON

The Watch Tower at Pilton, also known as the Bede House, is a most unusual piece of Northamptonshire's architecture. It was constructed around 1515 and at one time it was home to a curate and was also used as a grain store. From the gable on the northern end of the building, a slender watchtower with a pyramidal-shaped roof can be seen and flanking the second floor windows are vertical stone shafts which rise above small carved heads.

This tiny village, about four miles south of Oundle, stands close to the River Nene with Lilford Hall and Park beyond. The manor house was built in 1509, about six years before the Watch Tower, by a member of the Tresham family. It is a fine building with high, pointed gables and elegant windows, all surmounted by a series of tall, handsome chimneys.

Close by is the Church of St Mary and All Saints with its graceful spire standing atop the thirteenth-century tower. The south porch dates from the same period as the tower, while the rounded, arched doorway inside is undoubtedly Norman and has the tell-tale chevron design carved into its surface. Inside there is much to delight the eye from the thirteenth and fourteenth centuries, but also a great deal of adornment was added as recently as 1864 through the generosity of Lord Lilford.

Charlton.   C. Holmes

64. CHARLTON

Situated in the south of the county, not far from the north Oxfordshire border, is Charlton. It is a village without a parish church, which is rather unusual. The Church of St James is half a mile away at Newbottle. Little remains today of Newbottle except for a couple of cottages, the old rectory, the manor and the church; by contrast, Charlton is thriving.

Almost opposite the Rose and Crown in Main Street is a most unusual building. In the past it was the home of F.E. Smith, the first Earl of Birkenhead. He was a lawyer who rose to become Lord Chancellor of England, and he was also a friend of Winston Churchill. Moving here in 1907, he had the house extended until it became quite an imposing building, if a little unusual in appearance. The front door opens right onto the street, while at the rear, the gardens extend down to a small pond. Years ago, many of the village functions were held in this garden, including fêtes and tennis tournaments. On his death in 1930, F.E. Smith was buried in the cemetery, just to the west of the village, in a tomb designed by Lutyens.

Within the village there are numerous cottages and former farm buildings, many dating from the seventeenth and eighteenth centuries, which provide fine homes for their owners. The more recently built houses are mainly at the northern end of the village, while half a mile to the south is Rainsborough Camp, the ancient Iron Age hill fort.

The Chantry Chapel, Higham Ferrers.

65. THE MARKET SQUARE AND CHANTRY CHAPEL, HIGHAM FERRERS

Higham Ferrers was a thriving community back in Saxon times. Following the Norman Conquest, an early form of castle was constructed to the north of the church and by 1251 the Norman, William de Ferrers, had founded a borough with shops and a busy marketplace.

It was, however, Henry Chichele who brought fame to Higham Ferrers. He rose from obscurity to become Archbishop of Canterbury in 1414 and the remains of his Chichele College at Higham Ferrers are today in the care of English Heritage.

The Market Square, Higham Ferrers.

Just across the main road, the A5028, is the magnificent Church of the Blessed Virgin Mary, in front of which is the Chantry Chapel. Together with the striking old Bede House, they make up a fine array of medieval buildings. The distinction and quality of the group gives the impression that they have been plucked from a hidden part of Oxford and set down here in Northamptonshire, such is their aura.

The Bede House dates from 1428 and was constructed during Chichele's lifetime; it was home to twelve old men who received a penny a day pension. The building is most attractive, with alternate lines of limestone and ironstone.

The Chantry Chapel, shown here, was founded in 1422 and is a stately looking building with fine windows and parapets right up to its quite majestic pinnacles. Delicately carved flowers adorn the cornice, while the pinnacle, above the great west window, forms a canopy.

Following the Dissolution of the Monasteries by Henry VIII and the resultant suppression of the chantries, this fine old building became the school for the children of Higham Ferrers for many generations.

Harleston.

66. HARLESTONE

Everyone who travels on the A428 between Northampton and Rugby will recognise my illustration of the Fox and Hounds, formerly the Dusty Fox, with the beautiful, old, thatched stone cottages beyond. At this point, all the traffic heading north has slowed, having just passed the speed camera on the left. This then is today's view of Harlestone, but just over 250 years ago Bonnie Prince Charles and his army were stopped somewhere in the vicinity of Harlestone. Troops from Northamptonshire barred his advance towards London and his intended conquest of England. Thus, the uprising of the young pretender drew to a close.

Over more recent centuries the local area was a very important quarrying region, and the architecture of the nearby villages bear witness to the product of the 'hill and hollows' of the surrounding well-quarried countryside.

As a child living in the north-west of England, I never gave much thought to the source of the square block of stone which my grandmother used to clean her front step. It was here in Northamptonshire and certainly from Harlestone that the 'donkey stone' came. It could be bought at the local shops, but it was also given in exchange for unwanted household items by the rag and bone men, who during Victorian times toured the streets with their small donkey carts, hence the name 'donkey stone'.

67. STRIXTON

One of the tiniest hamlets in the county, Strixton consists of a sprinkling of former farmhouses and old cottages with the handsome Church Farm adjacent to the church.

Saddleback church towers are in short supply in Northamptonshire but here is one of them, a simple example of the builders' craft of 700 years ago. The church was restored during the nineteenth century and fortunately the building styles which were fashionable at that time were not imposed upon this old church, so it therefore appears today much as it did when originally constructed.

The church belfry is up in the saddleback tower and is accessed by way of a stone staircase built within the thickness of the stout stone walls. The west door dates from the fourteenth century and above it is an unusual circular window of six lights. The chancel screen is a little younger and dates from the fifteenth century, while the spiral altar rails are comparatively modern, having been installed during the seventeenth century.

Strixton Church.

St Peter's church and Church Road, Greatworth.

68. GREATWORTH

In the past, much of the meat that ended up on the dinner tables of London originated in Wales. The sheep and cattle that played a vital part in the feeding of the capital's residents were driven along certain old roads which ran from west to east through the border counties and through parts of Gloucestershire, Oxfordshire and Northamptonshire. One such drover's route lies just to the north of the village of Greatworth and no doubt the village, on its high vantage point, was developed many centuries ago due to its close proximity to this important route. Today, the picturesque village rightly deserves its conservation status, which was granted twenty years ago.

The fire of 1793 had a disastrous effect on the village, destroying many of the old records together with the manor house which was constructed on the site of an earlier house. The entrance to the earlier house was indicated by two finals carved in stone to represent a pair of pineapples, and it was from the earlier house that the village derives its connection with the New World.

The Pargiter family lived here from the time of Henry VIII when they acquired the manor. Amy, one of their daughters, married Laurence Washington of Sulgrave by whom she had eleven children, while John, Laurence's younger brother, married Dorothy Pargiter. Thus the connections with George Washington, the first President of the United States of America, were formed.

The viewpoint I have chosen for the illustration shows some of the attractive stone cottages in Church Road, with the small Church of St Peter beyond to the left. The church tower is fifteenth century in construction, while the chancel is 200 years older. The nave was almost completely rebuilt in the Early English style in 1882.

Not far from Greatworth, the Victorians built a railway junction to link the Banbury, Bletchley and Northampton lines. It was known as Cockley Brake. It was not a great commercial success and has long since passed into disuse.

69. STANION

To the east of the A43 and about three miles south-east of Corby, Stanion is positioned close by the Harper Brook and, in times gone by, the village was surrounded by the woods of the Forest of Rockingham. Today, the tall and elegant spire of the church looks down on the slate and thatched cottages which line the road to the west in the direction of Corby.

In the foreground of my illustration is the thatched Tithe Barn Cottage, beyond which is St Peter's Hall, with the fifteenth-century Church of St Peter the Apostle in the background. The church has a number of interesting features, not least of all its fifty or so carved heads which express various facial expressions and run around the top of the wall of the south aisle. In the middle of this collection is a large gargoyle carrying a water spout in his mouth. The south doorway is 700 years old and on each side of the nave are four arches dating from the fifteenth century. A wall painting depicts a unicorn, a stag and a cowled figure at prayer and the pulpit, of three-tier design, enables the preacher to look down on the congregation from his high vantage point. However, the most unusual possession must surely be the 'Dun Cow Rib'.

Many years ago, so the story goes, there was a large cow that provided milk for all the residents of Stanion and over a period of time the villages developed a great affection for the animal. A coven of local witches became so jealous of the animal that they decided to kill it! The whole of the village was horrified and in order to discourage any further visits to the village by the witches, they took a rib from the dead animal, had it consecrated and kept it in the church. The cow was buried with due ceremony beside the Corby road, the place being known as Cowthick.

Stanion.

70. THE LANTERN HOUSE, BADBY

About half a mile south of Badby, and standing beside the A361 road, is the old Lantern House. This two-storey, stone, octagonal building lay derelict for many years before being restored and renovated to provide a most charming house of distinction.

It is thought that the house dates originally from the early 1800s and is the work of Thomas Cundy. Standing on a high bank, it is surrounded by dense woodland which in springtime to early summer is carpeted with bluebells.

Unfortunately this building, a unique example of the architecture of yesteryear, is passed unnoticed by most who travel this route.

The Lantern House, Badby.

"Kunda Cottage", cob built with a roof of thatch. Lower Farm is beyond, Whilton.

71. WHILTON

Most readers will associate St Patrick with the Emerald Isle and not with Northamptonshire. Rumour has it, however, that St Patrick was born close to the village of Whilton. Bannaventa was the name of a Roman settlement on Watling Street which connected London to Holyhead and tales of the past tell that this 'saint to be' travelled first to Cornwall and then on to Ireland. Needless to say, there is nothing to substantiate this claim.

Almost at the centre of England, Whilton's importance grew during Roman times, but many centuries later, with the development of the traffic on the Grand Union Canal and with its famous flight of locks, Whilton developed further. During the days of coach travel it had become a staging post and today, with the service area of the M1 motorway not far away, history is to some extent repeating itself. The village has a pleasant blend of old cottages and houses, one of which is Dormer Cottage, dating from the late 1600s, which is said to have floorboards of timber which came from Northampton Prison. In front of the stone building is a later brick construction originally used as a music room. Many of the old village houses were formerly business premises or shops. During the eighteenth century, many of the residents of Whilton were employed in the wool trade and its related businesses. Wool combing, spinning, weaving and knitting were carried out here, as was shoemaking.

In England, many village schools were founded during early Victorian times, but in Whilton, a school was founded in farm buildings as early as 1768, thanks to the generosity of one Jonathan Emery. Mrs Worsfold was another benefactor who helped with the local education. She donated both money and land in 1815. The former large school house is now a private dwelling and behind it, the school room has become the Village Hall.

One of the most picturesque buildings in the village is of cob construction with a thatched roof, although it does have a gable end of brick. It is the white cottage in my illustration, beyond which are the former dairy buildings, now a private house called Lower Farm.

Before leaving Whilton, it is worth mentioning the church. It is a small, simple church with a squat, square tower. Dedicated to St Andrew, much restoration was carried out during the late eighteenth and nineteenth centuries. The church clock is unusual in that it is claimed to be Elizabethan in origin and only has forty-eight minutes on its face.

72. GRETTON

In the north of the county, close to the borders of Leicestershire and Rutland, and high above the beautiful Welland Valley, sits Gretton. It is a large village built on a hill and consists of a number of winding streets with handsome stone houses, tight corners and narrow lanes. Described by some writers as 'the fairest of villages', here fine houses, 200 to 300 years old, stand close to small cottages of similar age. Troubled times in the past are also brought to mind by the sight of the stocks up on the high village green.

Kirby Hall is only a couple of miles away. Now in the care of English Heritage, it is a beautiful Elizabethan ruin. Built in 1570 by Sir Humphrey Stafford, it was sold by his heir to Sir Christopher Hatton, the favourite of Elizabeth I. Over the centuries it was allowed to fall into ruin but now this dignified and classical piece of Elizabethan architecture is preserved for all to see.

Gretton's village church, dedicated to St James, is medieval in origin and has a fifteenth-century tower of brown stone which blends well with the grey stone of the nave and chancel. Parts of the church still retain their Norman origins in spite of the modifications made during the thirteenth and fourteenth centuries. The chancel dates from the eighteenth century and wall tablets remind us of the importance of the Hatton family in this part of Northamptonshire during the seventeenth and eighteenth centuries.

After centuries of being a self-contained community depending on local skills to sustain it, the coming of the railways during the early nineteenth century opened up the village and, like so many other places in rural England, Gretton people were able to travel outside their places of birth. Illustrated here are the picturesque old houses in Station Road, fine examples of the architecture that typifies the north of the county.

Station Road, Gretton.

Grendon Hall.

73. GRENDON

Like many villages in this beautiful county, Grendon is a mixture of various styles of small stone cottages and larger stone houses, many of which still retain their traditional roofs of thatch. However, other than the attractive dwellings of the village, Grendon has a hall which has a history of its own.

The Deputy Lieutenant of the Tower of London in 1685 was General Hatton Compton, who built the hall at Grendon on the site of an earlier building, and it was said to have been rebuilt again in 1720.

The Grand National is one of the main events of the horse racing calendar and in 1901, the winner, with the name of Grundon, was trained at Grendon Hall. When the great day dawned, the course had a covering of snow on it. In order to avoid getting bogged down, it was said that a pound of butter was placed on each of Grundon's hooves. This meant that the snow did not stick and it proved to be a wise investment.

During the Second World War, the hall was used by SOE (Special Operations Executive) and it seems that members of the 'Marquis', the resistance fighters of the Free French, were trained here.

Just after the war, on 29 July 1946, the then Princess Elizabeth opened the hall as a youth centre, only the second of its kind in the country. Today, many years later, it is a very successful residential youth centre with a multitude of courses run by Northamptonshire County Council.

The village church is dedicated to St Mary and looks out across the valley of the Nene. The tower displays a number of corbels and a pair of corbels with glaring expressions, said to represent husband and wife, are carved high on the chancel arch. The south doorway and the two western bays of the arcades are of Norman construction. The hatchments in the aisle are of the Compton family who resided at the hall. The ravens represent the arms of the Lord Lieutenant of the Tower and the connection with General Hatton Compton as Deputy.

74. SUTTON BASSETT

On a small ridge protruding into the Welland Valley, Sutton Bassett lies very close to the northern border of the county before the road takes the traveller into Leicestershire. From the edge of the village, fine views can be enjoyed and on a fine day it is said that if you know where to look, you may be able to count ten distant churches.

At the time of Domesday, the manor was held by the niece of William the Conqueror, the Countess Judith, and later by the Chief Justice of England, Richard Basset, from where the village undoubtedly derives its name. As with most villages there are modern houses here, but it is the old grey stone dwellings, many still having stone mullioned windows, which give the village its quaint charm. A few buildings have had brick-built additions at some time in their history, but this does not detract from their eye appeal. The village pub, the Queen's Head, is one such building and it was said to have been purchased in 1884 by a railway worker for £260.

At the village centre on the right of the road to Weston by Welland, the B664, is the tiny Church of All Saints. As you can see, it appears rather lonely, especially in winter. A simple yet graceful building, dating from Norman times, it was a chapel of ease and had no graveyard. It has an attractive bell cote and a Norman window in the chancel's north wall. A doorway into the nave is also Norman, as are the two round arches which are set upon stout columns to separate the south aisle from the nave. It is indeed a tranquil church in a pleasant little village.

Sutton Bassett.

75. FLORE

The old primary school, dated 1895 and situated in the south-west of the village surrounded by tall, leafless trees, caught my eye at Flore. It was famous in days gone by for its association with the May Day Festival and is said to have the names of the May Queens since the 1890s displayed on a board in one of its classrooms. Close by is the handsome old Jacobean manor house and next to it, the church. It seems that a settlement existed here long ago, close to the River Nene, for at the time of Domesday when it was known as Flora, there was a manor house and two mills along the river. Over the centuries the position of the village has shifted somewhat as the undulating land close to the church indicates that in the past the original village existed here. The recent development of the village, which started between the two world wars, was carried out on higher ground to the north of the busy A45 road.

The Church of All Saints is constructed of brown Northamptonshire stone and was mainly built during the thirteenth and fourteenth centuries. It has a stout tower with doors said to be about 600 years old. The font, dating from the sixteenth century, was discarded by the church and due to its barrel-like shape was used locally as a cattle trough. It was retrieved and entered the service of the Church of St Mary's at Dodford, where it stayed for some time before finding its way back here.

The Primary School, 1895, Flore.

Wicken Manor and church of St John.

76. WICKEN

Situated in the south-east of the county and quite close to Milton Keynes, Wicken was mentioned in the Domesday Book. Much later, during the thirteenth century, there were two parishes here, Wyke Hamoy or Hamon and Wyke Dyve, a small stream dividing the two, but in 1587 the parishes were combined.

Shown here, the manor house is to the left and close by is the fine old Church of St John. The tower contains a beam with the date 1621 and on the tower wall is a scratch dial from a time predating the invention of the clock. Most of the remainder of the church dates from the mid-eighteenth century and is in many ways typical of the architecture of that period. A wooden cross in the churchyard is said to be of medieval origin.

During the 1800s, Wicken Park was owned by Sir John Mordaunt and then later by Lord Penryhn, before it eventually became a private school.

Former business premises within the village, such as the bakers, the Post Office, the old forge and others, have long since been turned into fine private dwellings. The village also has a small number of houses dating from the Tudor period, one of which, opposite the old Post Office, was at some time in its history used as a hospital and as a prison.

77. EAST HADDON

A mill, a church and oxen for the plough were gifts from Leicester Abbey and all were recorded at the time of Domesday, together with three manors at 'Eddone'. Later the village became known as East Haddon, but still it was dependent on agriculture for its livelihood.

During the early nineteenth century, the village must have had a good water supply for there were twelve pumps and a couple of wells within easy access for the residents. Even today, one of the pumps still exists beneath its conical, thatched roof which is supported by six pillars. The pump stands at the corner of St Andrews Road with Walcot House beyond.

Today, East Haddon is a charming village of ironstone cottages, many of which are still thatched, while behind high iron gates stands the eighteenth-century hall. Mr Sawbridge who resided here was a great benefactor for the village for he, together with a group of like-minded people, financed the building of the village school and the school house for the school master. He also had a number of cottages constructed for his staff.

Close to the village centre stands St Mary's Church. Initially the building dates from Norman times, but much refurbishment was carried out during the fourteenth century. The chancel still retains its Norman pillars which support the chancel arch and the very attractive font is also from this period. The church tower was constructed during the fifteenth century and has pairs of windows with round heads, similar in style to Norman architecture.

The Old Water Pump, East Haddon.

Kiln Lane, Welton.

78. WELTON

Standing high up above the surrounding countryside and close to the border of Warwickshire, the village gets its name from the springs and wells which abound locally.

The local 'big house' in this vicinity was Welton Place, constructed during the eighteenth century by the Clarke family. A century or so later, a collection of rare trees and shrubs were planted surrounding their huge lake and today's humble border plant, the Clarkia, is accredited to this family who had a great interest in horticulture.

During more recent times the house became the residence of the Garrards, the Crown jewellers, and the family were often visited by members of the Royal family. Demolished about thirty years ago to make way for an estate of large houses, the excavations revealed many Roman artefacts, coins, pottery and human remains.

The village's Church of St Martin's has an unusual font. It is tub-shaped and is reputed to be Saxon, coming originally from East Anglia. The church dates from the thirteenth to sixteenth centuries and is essentially medieval. The pulpit, however, was carved by members of the village in 1899 and the poor box, with its outstretched hand, is from the same period.

Shown here is the view down Kiln Lane, with the old stone houses beside the road.

The Grand Union at Cosgrove.

79. COSGROVE

One of Northamptonshire's south eastern villages, Cosgrove, is just a few miles from central Milton Keynes in Buckinghamshire. The village still has a certain 'old world' charm and a number of links with the past.

Bounded by the Rivers Tove and Ouse, it became a settlement during Roman times but around 200 years ago its importance grew. Cosgrove found itself at the junction of the main canal linking London to Birmingham and the branch canal to Buckingham. Little of the latter arm remains today, but the Grand Union Canal brings numerous visitors in their narrow boats to the village during the summer months.

This view shows the former canal-side building high above the main street of Cosgrove. In the distance is the fourteenth-century tower of the Church of St Peter and St Paul, where the chancel dates from 1180. Captain Robert Moorsom was wounded at Trafalgar, survived and retired to Cosgrove, residing at the Priory, the 'grand' house of the village, for the latter part of his life. He and his wife are buried beneath the altar of this ancient church.

Close to the priory stood a water mill which was still in use until the 1920s but, alas, it has since been demolished. It was said that many years ago a daughter of the house fell in love with a local shepherd but as her family were opposed to the romance, he was deported to Australia on a false charge of sheep stealing. On learning of his fate, their daughter threw herself into the mill race and her ghost is said to haunt the area at full moon.

The Edward Hays boat building yards provided work at Cosgrove from 1840 to 1961 when all manner of tugs, launches and harbour vessels were built here, many of which were used all over the world.

Solomons Bridge No. 65, Cosgrove.

80. SOLOMONS BRIDGE (NO. 65), COSGROVE

When the Grand Junction Canal, the earlier name of the Grand Union Canal, was completed in 1800, it split the village of Cosgrove in two. The canal, being carried on a manmade bank high above the village, caused the former Main Street to be split in two. Today the eastern side is called Main Street and the western side is called The Stocks. The two halves are linked by a narrow passage at street level beneath the canal.

In order to maintain a road link to both parts of the village, a new route around the north of the village had to be constructed. The new route became Bridge Road and as a result of an agreement between the canal company and the owner of this land, the new road was carried over the canal by this elaborate Gothic-style bridge. It is no ordinary canal bridge. With its pointed arch, elaborate cut waters (these appear as supporting columns in this view) and its niches, one of which can be seen on the left, it certainly makes a handsome sight.

West Street, Kings Cliffe.

81. KINGS CLIFFE

Between the two world wars, ironstone quarrying ceased at Kings Cliffe. It is therefore no surprise that such a lot of it is in evidence in the older buildings along the narrow streets of this attractive village. As the very name Kings Cliffe suggests, it was, in the past, a royal manor and a place of some importance. At one time, it had a charter for a three-day fair and a weekly market.

During the ninetenth century the wood carving and wood turning trades developed here. Ten such craftsmen were listed in the village in 1874 and one of the former village inns was called the Turners Arms.

William Law (1686-1761) was a great village benefactor; he was the son of a grocer and became a clergyman of great standing. He founded the Law and Hutchinson Almshouses for six widows or single ladies. He also founded the William Law Library which is housed in the Library House on School Hill. The Carnforth Homes in Bridge Street are another example of village beneficiaries. These were endowed by a wealthy lady resident.

Arthingworth.

C. Holmes

82. ARTHINGWORTH

Arthingworth is a small village in the north-west of the county, a few miles south of Market Harborough. The view I have chosen shows the white cottage and the Church of St Andrew on the corner of Braybrooke Road.

The church sits high above the road junction and whilst it is thought to have late Norman origins, the nineteenth-century restorations are certainly more visible. The remains of a thirteenth-century South Chapel are also evident, but in the main it is obvious that much of the fabric of the building dates from fairly recent times.

Like many of Northamptonshire's villages, Arthingworth developed centuries ago as an agricultural village and had a number of large farms within the parish. Many of these former farmhouses, outbuildings and cottages have been modified and extended, and today provide very substantial homes for their occupants. In addition to agriculture, lacemaking was developed here during the mid-nineteenth century but its success was short-lived and the trade had almost disappeared after about twenty years.

83. YARDLEY GOBION

Enjoying a position in the south-east of the county, with the main A5 road to the west and the little River Tove and the Grand Union Canal over to the east, Yardley Gobion has expanded quite considerably during the last fifty years or so. During this period, old pottery kilns have been discovered, establishing the fact that during the fourteenth and fifteenth centuries it was a centre for a busy pottery industry.

Here the mixture of architectural styles makes the village so attractive. The view I have chosen is of the junction of the High Street and Moorend Road. To the right are the signpost and the village well which was refurbished and enclosed by the white fence for the Millennium.

Back in 1347, Edward III gave permission for Thomas de Ferrers to construct a castle with a surrounding moat at Moor End, but before the building was completed, twenty-two years later, the land reverted back to the Crown. It is known that the castle and manor still existed during the mid-1500s and during the English Civil War it was captured by the Parliamentarians. In time, its ownership passed back to Charles II. His son, the 1st Duke of Grafton, soon became the owner and Moor End stayed in the family's ownership until 1920.

84. GAYTON

Centuries ago, tales of strange 'goings-on' and of witches meant that Gayton had a rather forbidding aura about it. The gentleman after whom the village is named, Sir Philip de Gayton, had a daughter named Scholastica, who was said to have murdered her husband. She had a sister called Julianna, who bore a child known as Mabila. Julianna later met her fate by burning as it was decided that she was a witch. The facts of this tale have become somewhat confused over the centuries, but the de Gayton tombs are in the village church.

The Church of St Mary dates from the Norman period, as does the base of the tower, but the upper portion, modern by comparison, is nineteenth century. The circular font is also reputed to be Norman, but the remainder of the building was constructed during the Early English period.

The village stands on high ground a few miles south-west of Northampton, with the Grand Union Canal never far away, and the watershed of the Ouse and the Nene close by. The local ironstone gave a living to the villagers in the past when huge amounts were excavated from the surrounding countryside. No less than three brickyards also functioned here; they are all gone now and Gayton lives with its memories.

The handsome old manor house, close to the church, is seen here. It was built by Francis Tanfield during the early 1600s and has a certain similarity to the work of Sir Thomas Tresham at Lyveden New Bield. It was constructed in the shape of a cross, each arm ending with a gable in which are a series of graceful, stone mullioned windows on each of the three floors.

Yardley Gobion.

The Manor House, Gayton.

Wappenham.

85. WAPPENHAM

The older buildings in Wappenham are built of Helmdon stone while others of more recent construction are clearly of red brick. The village is without a large house, as it seems that at no time has there been a Lord of the Manor with a dwelling appropriate to that status.

This is still a small village with some recent development, but in the Middle Ages it was a humble clearing within the forest and had its own laws and certain privileges granted by the King. It probably developed due to its proximity to the old drovers' road, Welsh Lane, which crossed the Oxford Lane just to the north. The roads to Buckingham and Brackley were close by and the old Roman road, Watling Street, was not too distant. It is therefore of little surprise that inns grew up within the village providing accommodation for those who travelled through this part of Middle England. These have long since been converted to private dwellings and add to the charm of the present-day village.

At an intersection with the main road stands the Church of St Mary, with its fine pinnacle tower and wide chancel. It dates from the thirteenth century, and inside are brasses which commemorate the Lovatts, the residents of Astwell Manor, a fortified house dating from 1520. The brasses are said to have been repositioned here from the abbey of Bittlesden following the Dissolution of the Monasteries by Henry VIII.

Adjacent to the church, but unfortunately hidden behind a high wall, is the handsome old rectory, dated 1832. It is the work of Gilbert Scott, who also designed the village school and a number of other properties in the village. These stout stone houses stand almost facing the church, close to the curve in the High Street.

Finally, here is an amusing tale for the reader, but not so for the guilty party of four centuries ago. It concerns one Theophilus Hart, who had an eye for the ladies and who, at that time, was involved in an extramarital affair with the wife of the village butcher. Unfortunately for Theophilus, the butcher was alerted to the romantic goings-on of his wife and he decided that he had to teach Theophilus a lesson. The story tells of the butcher chasing him across the countryside until finally he caught and killed him with his butcher's knife. Later it was found that Theophilus, the ardent lover, had been a man of sixty-five years of age.

The Green, where the High Street meets School Lane, Eydon.

86. EYDON

Situated in the south of the county and close to its western edge, Eydon is well positioned on a slight hill and is surrounded by undulating wooded countryside.

It is thought that the village may have had its origins during Roman times when it developed beside a road linking Daventry with Chipping Warden, but it is certain that Eydon was recorded at the time of Domesday in 1086 and possibly it was a Saxon settlement even before that time. Today's village dates mainly from the seventeenth and eighteenth centuries and consists of various lovely, old stone buildings lining the High Street, but being interspersed with many noble-looking trees. Some of the buildings are set back from the street but many front right onto it, mainly private buildings now, but in days gone by many would have been business premises, the very infrastructure to support a rich village such as Eydon.

At one end of the High Street, after a sharp right-hand bend, the road joins School Lane close to the Green; it is this junction that I have chosen to illustrate. Behind the viewer are the old stocks and the entrance to the hall designed by James Lewis and built around 1790 for the Revd Francis Annesley, who is commemorated in the nearby church.

It is believed that a church has stood at Eydon since 1154, but it has been renovated over the centuries, particularly in 1864-65. Much survives from the earlier architectural periods; the squat tower, for instance, is fourteenth century. The pillars in the north arcade are Norman and they support fourteenth-century arches, while in the vestry the effigy of the lady is said to be the wife of Sir Richard Wale, Lord of the Manor during the reign of Edward II.

In the past, the village suffered two fires; one took place in 1651 and the other as recently as 1905. Certain buildings in the village still retain their scorch marks from these terrible events. During more recent times, the development of the nearby railways brought some prosperity to the village but by 1966 the last train ran locally and all was quiet once again at Eydon.

87. STANWICK

A short distance to the north-east of Higham Ferrers is the village of Stanwick, standing on high ground overlooking the River Nene. The village is dominated by the octagonal tower and spire of the Church of St Lawrence.

This is the viewpoint from the car park, close to the church, where the elegance of the 153ft-high spire, with its three gabled openings on alternate sides, can clearly be seen. Below the spire, the belfry has a series of window arches above which is a delicately carved frieze and inside the belfry, one of the bells is dated 1360. With its priest's room above the entrance porch, the Church of St Lawrence is certainly one of the finest examples of Early English church architecture in the county.

Inside the church, the pulpit dates from the sixteenth century and was given to the church by John Dolben. He was a Royalist who fought and was wounded at the Battle of Marston Moor and was one of those who defended the city of York when it was besieged by General Fairfax. Following the defeat of the King and the end of the Civil War, he returned to the church, for his father had been the rector here. He studied hard and later became the Bishop of Rochester and eventually Bishop of York where, on his death, he was buried.

Church of St Lawrence, Stanwick.

88. HARRINGTON

At Harrington, the Church of St Peter and St Paul, originally dedicated to St Botolph, is not in the village as is normally the case, but a short distance away down the lane to Thorpe Underwood. It is now a listed building and dates mainly from the fourteenth and fifteenth centuries, with renovations being carried out during the early part of the nineteenth century. During this period the tower was added at the end of the south transept. Inside, the aisles and arcades date from the fourteenth century, as does the canopied screen with its delicately carved details of grapes and leaves of the vine. The Saunders family is well-represented with a marble monument from 1545, together with portraits in brass and a wall-mounted monument of 1588.

The item common to Braybrooke and to Harrington is kept in the church and is known as 'the Vamping Horn'. A curious brass instrument, about 5ft in length, its use was similar to a megaphone, to 'vamp up' sound. It was used to make a loud humming noise to accompany the choir and was so efficient that it could be heard a mile away, and so it was also used to call the villagers to worship. It seems that very few of these instruments exist today; it is therefore unusual that the two which survive in Northamptonshire are in this part of the county. Buried in the churchyard of St Peter and St Paul are a number of those slain at the Battle of Naseby, and close by the church are a series of terraces and mounds, sadly all that remains today of the grandeur of the old manor house.

The Tollemache Arms and Church Farm, Harrington.

It was known as Arintone at the time of the Domesday Book, but over the centuries this has become Harrington. Falls Field, at the village centre, was once the site of a monastic manor owned by the Knights Hospitaller of St John of Jerusalem. Since those days it has been laid out as an ornamental garden with fish ponds, terraces and sunken gardens.

Finally, I must mention an amusing story about the village pub, the Tollemache Arms, shown here. In 1870 and at the age of eighty-seven, the rector of Harrington, the Revd Hugh Tollemache, passed away. He had served the community well for fifty-eight years and during his time in the village had acquired a certain reputation for his determination to have his will done. He had taken umbrage at his parishioners' habit of visiting the pub on the Sabbath day and so when the opportunity to purchase the business became available, he grabbed the chance. This done, he installed his faithful coachman as landlord and gave him express instructions that the inn was only to be opened six days a week and must be closed on the Sabbath day. Since then it has been known as the Tollemache Arms and at present is open seven days a week.

The Dovecote, Upper Harlesdon.

Maidwell.

89. MAIDWELL

Maidwell straddles the main A508 road a few miles south of Market Harborough. It was mentioned in the Domesday Book and indeed, there was a settlement in the vicinity during the Iron Age and the Roman period.

During the 1500s, the manor was divided into two main houses and two churches, which was quite unusual. The Church of St Peter, together with one of the manor houses, seems to have disappeared over the centuries, although the house may be part of Manor Farm. To the east of the main road is Maidwell Hall, possibly the second manor house and today a well-known school.

This view is one familiar to all who travel the road north from Brixworth towards Market Harborough. On the left is the picturesque Stag's Head, with the Old House on the right of the road just beyond the bus stop.

The narrow lane that meanders eastwards, just to the south of this viewpoint, contains some of the former buildings of the old village. The former bakehouse, Post Office and the old school house are all now private houses. The old rectory and rectory farmhouse, together with the Church of St Mary the Virgin, are all close by. A plain Norman arch in the south doorway and some work of the same period inside the tower give an indication of the age of St Mary's in spite of most of the fabric dating from the thirteenth century.

90. THE DOVECOTE, UPPER HARLESTONE

Not too distant from Duston, on the outskirts of Northampton and close to Althorp Park, lies the tiny hamlet of Upper Harlestone. For centuries, Harlestone has had a close association with the great house of Althorp and the Spencer family.

Immediately after a sharp bend in the road on the north-western edge of the village, the circular dovecote shown in my illustration comes into view. This charming old building stands in a cottage garden surrounded by trees, shrubs and flowers. Its walls are about 3ft thick and it is about 15ft high. It had nesting places for about 400 pairs of birds when it was designed and built during the fifteenth century. At this time a special servant, known as the columbarius, would be responsible for the birds housed in such dovecotes, who were encouraged to breed in order to provide food for the family of the manor house.

This viewpoint of the Dovecote and the Dovecote Laundry will be familiar to all who travel through Upper Harlestone.

St Margaret's church and Roundhouse Cottage, Alderton.

91. ALDERTON

Driving south along the main A508 road from Northampton, the road has a number of steep bends before crossing the Grand Union Canal at Stoke Bruerne; then comes a long straight before the hill at Grafton Regis. At the bottom of the hill is the sign to Alderton, a tiny hamlet of attractive dwellings amidst fields and woodland.

At the time of Domesday, it was known as Alritone and later Aldrington, and according to old records the 'manor house stood in a low position at the north-west extremity of the village'. It was described as a very large mansion house which at one time was acquired by Henry VIII. In 1605, Queen Anne of Denmark was entertained there for four nights, and three years later King James visited it. During later centuries it had various owners, but eventually fell into disrepair.

As recently as 1831, the records show that the village had thirty-six houses and 162 inhabitants, and today it remains an attractive village with its pretty cottages and the small Perpendicular-style Church of St Margaret, which was largely rebuilt by 1848 with the exception of the fifteenth-century tower. Inside the church is an early fourteenth-century wooden effigy of Sir William de Coumbemartin, who it is thought was the former Lord of the Manor and who died in 1318.

Whilst the presence of a castle at Alderton had been acknowledged for centuries, it was assumed that the remains had become overgrown and tree-covered over the years. It was generally thought that it might have been a medieval building under a mound not far from the church. During the Millennium year, the television show *Time Team* visited Alderton to attempt to clarify the origins of the castle mound and possibly date it. At the close of their survey it was decided that below the mound at Alderton, there once stood a Norman castle of the ring work design and, unlike the more common type of Norman structure of motte and bailey, it was devoid of a motte. It consisted in the main of a flattened mound with buildings on top of it. Possibly it dated from the early years following the Norman Conquest, or it might have been from a century later, during the dark days of the wars between King Stephen and Matilda. It is a colourful past for a quiet hamlet.